# Parallel Spelling Tests

## second edition

## Dennis Young

**Hodder & Stoughton**
A MEMBER OF THE HODDER HEADLINE GROUP

# Year Groups

In this handbook, the Year-groups referred to are those in England and Wales. Equivalent year-groups in Scotland and in Northern Ireland are:

| England & Wales | Scotland | Northern Ireland |
|---|---|---|
| Reception (R) | P1 | Y1 |
| Year 1 | P2 | Y2 |
| Year 2 | P3 | Y3 |
| Year 3 | P4 | Y4 |
| Year 4 | P5 | Y5 |
| Year 5 | P6 | Y6 |
| Year 6 | P7 | Y7 |
| Year 7 | S1 | Y8 |

ISBN 0 340 73093 5
Second edition 1998
Impression number   10 9 8 7 6 5 4 3 2 1
Year   2004  2003  2002  2001  2000  1999  1998

Copyright © 1983, 1998 D. Young

All rights reserved. No part of this publication may be reproduced or transmitted in any form or by any means, electronic or mechanical, including photocopy, recording or any information storage and retrieval system, without permission in writing from the publisher. *This publication is excluded from the reprographic licensing scheme administered by the Copyright Licensing Agency Ltd.*

Printed in Great Britain for Hodder & Stoughton Educational, a division of Hodder Headline Plc, 338 Euston Road, London NW1 3BH, by Hobbs the Printers Ltd, Totton, Hants.

# Contents

| | |
|---|---|
| Spelling in the National Curriculum and National Literacy Strategy | 4 |
| Introduction | 5 |
| Preparing a Spelling Test | 6 |
| Administering a Spelling Test | 6 |
| Marking | 7 |
| Using the Tables of Norms | 7 |
| **Spelling Tests A: Infants and Lower Juniors** | 8 |
| *Table One: Tests A Quotients. Year 2* | *16* |
| *Table Two: Tests A Quotients. Year 3* | *17* |
| *Table Three: Tests A Quotients. Year 4* | *18* |
| *Table Four: Tests A Spelling Ages* | *19* |
| **Spelling Tests B: Upper Juniors and Secondary Pupils** | 20 |
| *Table Five: Tests B Quotients. Year 5* | *29* |
| *Table Six: Tests B Quotients. Years 6 and 7* | *30* |
| *Table Seven: Tests B Spelling Ages* | *31* |
| Examining the Results and Extending the Assessments | 32 |
| Learning from Children's Spelling Errors | 34 |
| Construction and Investigations | 36 |
| *Statistics* | *39* |
| References | 40 |

# Spelling in the National Curriculum and National Literacy Strategy

The National Curriculum for English at Key Stages 1 and 2 identifies spelling as a Key Skill in Attainment Target 3: Writing. The Programmes of Study emphasise the importance of children learning to spell a range of increasingly complex words; Level Descriptions define a series of steps in this progression, from simple, monosyllabic words at Level 2 to words with complex regular patterns at Level 5.

Within this range, the Programmes of Study specify that children should be taught to spell words with particular features. At Key Stage 1, the focus is on commonly occurring words and words with simple spelling patterns, common letter strings, and common prefixes and suffixes. At Key Stage 2, this is extended to include work on word families, roots and origins; alternative ways of spelling the same sound; words with inflectional endings; complex polysyllabic words, and words with silent letters.

The National Literacy Strategy Framework for Teaching (DFEE 1998) lists spelling as a general literacy objective, stating that *'primary pupils should understand the sound and spelling system and use this to read and spell accurately'*. The word-level strand of the framework includes termly objectives for spelling which specify the spelling patterns and word parts to be taught. Appendices list high- and medium-frequency words which children should be able not only to recognise on sight in their reading but also be able to spell correctly. These objectives closely follow the National Curriculum Programmes of Study, providing a more detailed and systematic guide for the teaching and assessment of spelling. The Framework for Teaching also emphasises the importance of children acquiring explicit knowledge of the complex relationship between letters and sounds in English and of word structure, including much work on roots, prefixes, suffixes and inflections.

The **Parallel Spelling Tests** reflect the model of progression and the word types specified in the National Curriculum and the National Literacy Strategy. Early levels of the test focus on words with simple, regular spelling patterns and on commonly occurring words. Successive levels include a range of words with increasingly complex patterns. These include: words with prefixes and suffixes (for example, *wooden, pretend, repair, careful, suddenly, alteration*); words with inflectional endings (for example, *pushing, entered, dancing, knives*); words with silent letters (for example, *talk, castle, island, whisper, sword*); and words which exemplify the range of spelling patterns for long vowel phonemes (for example, *money, dream, angry, these, steeple*).

Because of these similarities in content and progression, the **Parallel Spelling Tests** offer an effective and useful way of measuring attainment in spelling in relation to the requirements of the National Curriculum and the National Literacy Strategy Framework for Teaching. The standardised results, expressed in Spelling Quotients and Spelling Ages, provide a summative indication of attainment referenced to national norms; these can also be used to measure and compare progression within the school year by year.

Close examination of test results will also yield evidence which can serve a *formative* purpose. In particular, such an examination can reveal the types of words and spelling patterns that are causing difficulties at individual, class or whole-school levels. For example, it may show that children tend to spell incorrectly words with inflectional endings or with less common spelling patterns for long vowels. (For more information on the examination and interpretation of children's spelling errors, see page 32.) By highlighting areas of strength and weakness, such evidence can help teachers target future teaching more accurately and may even suggest changes to a school's policy and schemes of work for spelling.

In these ways, the **Parallel Spelling Tests** can help teachers and schools bring both the assessment and the teaching of spelling into line with the requirements of the National Curriculum and the National Literacy Strategy Framework for Teaching.

# Introduction

The **Parallel Spelling Tests** are presented in two banks of items. From each of these banks, parallel tests can be formed, one bank being suitable for Years 2 to 4, and the other for Years 5 to 7. A total of twelve matched tests without overlap (and a much larger number with partial overlap) are then available for charting the progress of children for over six years. The tables of quotient norms range from age 6:5 to 12:11 and the spelling ages from 6 to 15 years.

Spelling is important because of its part in efficient written communication, and it would be most satisfactory if spelling could be judged (as it is in business and social correspondence) in context. However, assessing children's spelling from their written work is a laborious and uncertain process.

There is, of course, another test of spelling competence which is applied in everyday affairs. Among adults, the 'good speller' is the friend or colleague who can be relied upon to answer the question '*How do you spell . . . ?*' Dictated word spelling tests are valid by this model.

There is a positive correlation between assessments from children's writing and from dictated word spelling tests, and each approach should be regarded as providing valid information which can be used to complement and enhance the other in the assessment of children's strengths and weaknesses, not only in spelling, but in the integration of writing skills.

The dictated word type of spelling test compares well with other objective tests of spelling (Freyberg 1970) and can be conveniently adapted to the 'bank' system, which has several advantages:

- the abundance of the material and the flexibility with which a large number of different (but matched) tests can be formed by the user render the results less vulnerable to practice effects and coaching;
- checking initial results or systematically increasing the reliability of scores by further testing presents no difficulty.

Assurance of the strict comparability of a series of results is, of course, of vital importance when children are being tested at intervals, whether yearly or at shorter intervals, as for example when a child is receiving special help.

A further practical advantage for the user is that the number of items to be attempted is determined by the age group of the children and not by successive *ad hoc* extensions of the test to include words suitable for small groups of less and more able children. No assumed or estimated adjustments to the raw scores are necessary before consulting the tables or norms.

The items are presented in complete sentences so that the preparations are minimal. According to the age of the pupils, the test is taken either from Tests A or Tests B. One pair of sentences is selected from each of the successive groups of six pairs to form a test of the prescribed length for the age group.

Each test takes approximately 20 minutes to administer and is quickly marked.

Yearly use of standardised tests provides a conveniently concise and accurate core of hard information for school records. Reviews of the results, combined with the teacher's observations, may lead to insights that might otherwise be missed. Contrasting achievements in spelling and reading may in some cases be of particular interest. The freedom with which a child writes is certainly affected to some degree (depending partly on temperament, perhaps) by his or her confidence in their own spelling ability.

Such reviews (as illustrated in the section *Examining the Results and Extending the Assessments*) also ensure that children whose need for special assistance has not been detected in the course of the year will be considered for further investigation within the school and, it may be, for referral to some specialist – special needs teacher, adviser or educational psychologist.

*Examining the Results and Extending the Assessments* is followed by a section on *Learning from Children's Spelling Errors*.

The section *Construction and Investigations* presents considerable evidence for the accuracy of the sampling used for the standardisations, and reports correlations with other tests over a wide age range. These also show reliability coefficients with a mean of 0.94 for both Tests A and B.

The practical advantages of the format, combined with the satisfactory technical backing, make the **Parallel Spelling Tests** highly suitable for use by teachers, educational psychologists and research workers.

The construction of these tests has been supported by the continued interest and cooperation of hundreds of teachers. A number of headteachers and class teachers also made helpful comments on the initial draft of the sections of teaching. For obvious reasons it is impossible either to list all names or to produce a more limited list. All are offered further thanks.

The author is also grateful to Peter Bell, Derek Clark, Sue Knight, Geoff Lindsay, Alan MacAuslan, Maurice Peterson and Vera Quin for valuable comments on a first draft of some sections. It is hoped that all their criticisms have been accommodated, but this does not guarantee their unreserved support for this final version.

# Preparing a Spelling Test

There are two banks of items, A and B. Bank A is for use with Years 2 to 4 (ages 6:4 to 9:11); bank B is for use with Years 5 to 7 (ages 9:0 to 12:11).

Both banks are divided into sections, each of which contains six pairs of items. The procedure for forming a test is the same for both banks. One pair of items is selected from each of the successive sections until the advised limit is reached. For reasons explained in the section *Construction and Investigations*, pairs should not be split.

| Group | Bank | Pairs | Items |
|---|---|---|---|
| Year 2 | A | 17 | 34 |
| Year 3 | A | 20 | 40 |
| Year 4 | A | 23 | 46 |
| Year 5 | B | 22 | 44 |
| Year 6 and Secondary pupils | B | 25 | 50 |

The advised limits of the tests listed above (34 items for Year 2, etc.) are indicated in the item banks.

If the test is being formed by the class teacher, the best way of avoiding any bias is by some predetermined routine. Simply write a series of numbers between 1 and 6 such as 4, 6, 1, 5, etc., and take the fourth pair from the first section, the sixth pair from the second section, and so on. Specialist users of the tests who wish to select according to some preferred set of spelling patterns may do so without invalidating the norms.

The suggested sentences can be changed if the user wishes to do this, but the procedure (dictation of the word, sentence, dictation of the word) must be adhered to.

Marking time can be saved if the pupils' answer papers follow a uniform pattern, i.e. so that the column numbers correspond from paper to paper. Duplicated sheets providing numbered lines, a place for names, etc., save time in administration, and confusion in the course of the testing. Younger children are of course particularly likely to make slips when asked to number their own papers and this is not always detected before beginning the testing, but older children are not immune from this kind of frustrating error. A4 paper turned to make a base on a long side can be conveniently numbered in five columns of increasing width, 1 to 10, 11 to 20, ... 41 to 50.

# Administering a Spelling Test

Remove or cover potentially helpful posters or wall displays (word lists, etc.).

If the test is being administered to a large group, precautions against copying may need to be taken – e.g. tables may need separating.

Ensure that each pupil has a pencil and that spares are available. As marking problems arise from lack of legibility, explain the need for good writing while the pupils are writing their names – and remind them again in the course of the test. Do not ask them to use capitals.

Each item is presented as shown in the item banks, i.e. by giving the number of the item, the word to be spelt, the sentence embodying the word and, finally, the word again.

With younger children, it is advisable initially to check that the words are being written against the correct prepared numbers. Checking is also necessary because some children write more than the required word until corrected. The time available for each item (including the sentence and repetition) should be about 20 seconds, i.e. the time for forty items should be about 14 minutes. For the older children, the simpler items can be presented at the rate of one every 15 seconds and the most difficult items at the rate of one every 25 to 30 seconds.

The aim is to allow sufficient time for slow writers who know how to spell the words, but not enough for pupils to make several attempts.

Delivery should be slower and more distinct than in normal conversation. Special care should be taken with final consonants, but vowels should not be changed to indicate the spelling. This obviously applies to the vowels which occur in many unaccented syllables – e.g. pass*age*, surf*ace*, tort*oise*, wood*en*, etc.

There is little point in persisting with a 34-item test with those infants in a test group who are out of range of any possible success. Such children should be diverted to some other occupation which has been previously prepared. The same guidance applies to the testing of some older children, but care is needed since there is always the danger that a cut-off dictated too much by the teacher's anticipations may be premature, with consequent distortion of the total scores.

# Marking

Such difficulties as there are in marking a spelling test usually arise from poor handwriting. Where it is clear – either from examination of the other words on the spelling answer paper or from knowledge of the children's handwriting – that the doubt arises merely from poor handwriting, credit should be allowed. If the doubt cannot be cleared up, then the answer should be marked wrong. A correct sequence of letters is marked right despite any reversals or inversions of the individual letters. Whenever possible, try to resolve any doubts by asking the child to read back the reversed, inverted or badly-written letters.

Marking errors sometimes occur when children have replaced the required word with another, correctly spelt, word. Such words tend to be credited unless the marker is using a checklist placed next to the pupil's answers for constant reference.

# Using the Tables of Norms

The raw scores can be converted to spelling ages and to quotients. **Spelling ages** correspond more directly to teachers' own impressions of the children's relative ability; they are more easily interpreted in practical terms (spelling ages about 8 years indicating competence at average Year 3 level, etc.) and they more accurately suggest viable groups for remedial work.

**Quotients** show the relative positions of children who are, within a month, the same age. The quotients are calculated to divide a large typical group of children in the way shown in the following table.

| Quotient | Percentage above | Percentage below |
|---|---|---|
| 130 | 2½ | 97½ |
| 120 | 9 | 91 |
| 110 | 25 | 75 |
| 100 | 50 | 50 |
| 90 | 75 | 25 |
| 80 | 91 | 9 |
| 70 | 97½ | 2½ |

It must not be assumed that these percentages apply, or should apply, to all schools; there are considerable variations from area to area according to socio-economic conditions and other factors.

Quotients incorporating an age allowance are a useful way of checking impressions of the abilities of those children who, because they are younger, tend to be underestimated within the class. The youngest child may be below average when compared with other children in the class, but he may be above average compared with children of precisely the same age. For this reason, quotients may be more suitable for school records. After a lapse of time, a spelling age has less value unless care is taken to judge it in relation to the child's chronological age at the time of the test. A quotient does this automatically. For the same reason, comparison with tests taken at other times is easier if the results are in quotient form.

If **quotients** are required, it is necessary first to work out the chronological ages of the children. These should be in years and completed months, as in the following examples:

|  | Day | Month | Year |
|---|---|---|---|
| Date of test | 17 | 6 | 99 |
| Date of birth | 18 | 8 | 90 |
| Age | 30 | 9 | 8 |

Age in completed months: 8 years 9 months

If many ages have to be worked out, then the work can be reduced by a procedure which gives, for any test date, a simple rule or table. First work out the two possibilities for children born in August. If the date of the test is 17 June 1999 (as in the foregoing example), then the children born between 18 and 31 August 1990 will be 8:9, and those born between 1 and 17 August will be 8:10. From this table can be written:

| Date of birth | Age |
|---|---|
| 18–31 August | 8:9 |
| 1–17 August | 8:10 |
| 18–31 July | 8:10 |
| 1–17 July | 8:11 |
| etc. | etc. |

Now turn to Table 1 (for Year 2), Table 2 (for Year 3) Table 3 (for Year 4), Table 5 (for Year 5), or Table 6 (for Years 6 and 7).

Find the intersection of the column corresponding to the age and the row corresponding to the raw score. If the score leads to a quotient outside the limits of the table, record a quotient of greater than (>) 135 or less than (<) 70.

The term 'quotient' is used here as a more familiar substitute for 'standardised score'. Traditional quotients obtained by dividing spelling ages by chronological ages (a method still repeated in some out-of-date texts) can grossly confuse assessments.

For Tests A **spelling ages**, turn to Table 4 and select the column according to the number of items used in the test, i.e. 34, 40 or 46. Similarly, for Tests B, turn to Table 7 and use the 44-item or 50-item norms as appropriate.

# SPELLING TESTS A

*Year 2, 34 words.    Year 3, 40 words.    Year 4, 46 words.*

1. **In**  Put the pencils in the box.   Write **In**
2. **Men**  The men were working on the roads.   Write **Men**

1. **Man**  A boy grows up to be a man.   Write **Man**
2. **At**  The postman came at 9 o'clock.   Write **At**

1. **It**  It was raining in the night.   Write **It**
2. **Get**  The prisoner tried to get over the wall.   Write **Get**

1. **Me**  I saw the letter was for me.   Write **Me**
2. **Got**  He got a pencil from the box.   Write **Got**

1. **Is**  Morning is the time before noon.   Write **Is**
2. **On**  Boats sail on the sea.   Write **On**

1. **We**  We sleep during the night.   Write **We**
2. **Up**  The boy climbed up the rope.   Write **Up**

---

3. **Hat**  The wind blew the man's hat off.   Write **Hat**
4. **Run**  He will run as fast as he can.   Write **Run**

3. **Can**  Some birds can swim.   Write **Can**
4. **Bus**  The bus was carrying only two passengers.   Write **Bus**

3. **Fox**  The hounds chased the fox.   Write **Fox**
4. **He**  Jim said he was going.   Write **He**

3. **Red**  Some roses are red.   Write **Red**
4. **Fat**  The meat had too much fat on it.   Write **Fat**

3. **Ran**  The girl ran well in the race.   Write **Ran**
4. **Go**  After work, most people go straight home.   Write **Go**

3. **Yes**  The opposite of 'no' is 'yes'.   Write **Yes**
4. **Gun**  The soldier had a gun.   Write **Gun**

---

5. **Leg**  David hurt his leg while playing football.   Write **Leg**
6. **Cap**  A cap is one kind of hat.   Write **Cap**

5. **Jam**  Jam is made from fruit.   Write **Jam**
6. **End**  She sat at the end of the row.   Write **End**

5. **Pet**  He kept a rabbit as a pet.   Write **Pet**
6. **My**  He said, 'I have lost my coat as well.'   Write **My**

5. **Let**  The doorman let him go in.   Write **Let**
6. **Fog**  It is hard to see in a fog.   Write **Fog**

5. **Boy**  A boy delivered the papers.   Write **Boy**
6. **Set**  He set off to walk.   Write **Set**

5. **Lot**  A lot of people watch television.   Write **Lot**
6. **Pig**  The farmer had a pig to sell.   Write **Pig**

# SPELLING TESTS A

7. **This**  This cake is better than that cake.  Write **This**
8. **Be**  Be careful crossing the road.  Write **Be**

7. **Wet**  The rain will wet her hair.  Write **Wet**
8. **Land**  Australia is a far-off land.  Write **Land**

7. **Rug**  There was a rug on the floor.  Write **Rug**
8. **Went**  They went to London on the train.  Write **Went**

7. **Well**  The patient became well again.  Write **Well**
8. **Toy**  From the aeroplane, the car looked like a toy.  Write **Toy**

7. **Cow**  The cow came to be milked.  Write **Cow**
8. **Will**  They will go to the shop tomorrow.  Write **Will**

7. **Gas**  Some cookers use gas.  Write **Gas**.
8. **Ship**  A sailor works on a ship.  Write **Ship**

9. **Then**  First he walked and then he ran.  Write **Then**
10. **Make**  Road drills make a noise.  Write **Make**

9. **From**  We get bread from a shop.  Write **From**
10. **Cake**  A birthday cake has icing on it.  Write **Cake**

9. **Left**  He took the turning to the left.  Write **Left**
10. **Flat**  The family lived in a flat.  Write **Flat**

9. **Trap**  The poacher set a trap.  Write **Trap**
10. **Came**  Great crowds came to the match.  Write **Came**

9. **Fish**  Tuna is one kind of fish.  Write **Fish**
10. **Tent**  Campers use a tent.  Write **Tent**

9. **Flag**  The Union Jack is a flag.  Write **Flag**
10. **Soft**  Cushions are soft.  Write **Soft**

11. **Best**  The shoes were the best she could buy.  **Best**
12. **Melt**  When the sun comes out, the snow will melt.  Write **Melt**

11. **Lamp**  You should have a lamp on your bicycle.  Write **Lamp**
12. **Fist**  To make a fist you close your hand.  Write **Fist**

11. **Down**  The ball rolled down the hill.  Write **Down**
12. **Just**  The rescuers arrived just in time.  Write **Just**

11. **Must**  You must be careful with electricity.  Write **Must**
12. **Help**  Road signs help drivers.  Write **Help**

11. **Step**  In the dark, you must mind your step.  Write **Step**
12. **Much**  She did not like chocolate very much.  Write **Much**

11. **Stop**  They waited for the bus to stop.  Write **Stop**
12. **Very**  Ice-cream is very cold.  Write **Very**

# SPELLING TESTS A

13. **Boat** The man wanted a boat to go fishing. Write **Boat**
14. **Crisp** Biscuits should be crisp. Write **Crisp**

13. **Coat** His thick coat kept him warm. Write **Coat**
14. **Stamp** A letter needs a stamp. Write **Stamp**

13. **Farm** We bought eggs at the farm. Write **Farm**
14. **String** String is used to tie things together. Write **String**

13. **Over** Aeroplanes fly over the ocean. Write **Over**
14. **Start** He wanted to start a business. Write **Start**

13. **Town** The farmer went shopping in the town. Write **Town**
14. **Never** He never watches television. Write **Never**

13. **Cold** In winter it is cold. Write **Cold**
14. **Sharp** Razors have to be sharp. Write **Sharp**

---

15. **Drive** To drive a car, you must have a licence. Write **Drive**
16. **Paper** Books are made from paper. Write **Paper**

15. **Round** A ball is round. Write **Round**
16. **Danger** Rocks are a danger to ships. Write **Danger**

15. **Garden** She grows flowers in her garden. Write **Garden**
16. **Butter** Butter is made from milk Write **Butter**

15. **Letter** The postman brought a letter. Write **Letter**
16. **Found** Shells are found on beaches. Write **Found**

15. **Pushing** Pushing a pram can be hard work. Write **Pushing**
16. **Gather** Farmers gather the harvest in the autumn. Write **Gather**

15. **House** A house has a roof. Write **House**
16. **Dinner** They cleared the table after dinner. Write **Dinner**

---

17. **Drink** Cats drink milk. Write **Drink**
18. **Front** The front door is on the street side. Write **Front**

17. **Nothing** A man who has lost everything has nothing. Write **Nothing**
18. **Wooden** A cook sometimes uses a wooden spoon. Write **Wooden**

17. **Train** She travelled by train to London. Write **Train**
18. **Silver** Silver is a precious metal. Write **Silver**

17. **First** The first runner to the tape is the winner. Write **First**
18. **Donkey** He paid to ride on a donkey. Write **Donkey**

17. **Thank** You must thank people for their presents. Write **Thank**
18. **Money** She kept her money in a purse. Write **Money**

17. **Rabbit** A rabbit has long ears. Write **Rabbit**
18. **Queen** The queen attends ceremonies. Write **Queen**

# SPELLING TESTS A

19. **Ground**   He stumbled and fell to the ground.   Write **Ground**
20. **Month**   January is the first month of the year.   Write **Month**

19. **Talk**   Some parrots can talk.   Write **Talk**
20. **Uncle**   My mother's brother is my uncle.   Write **Uncle**

19. **Mouth**   The dog took the bone in its mouth.   Write **Mouth**
20. **Fight**   Dogs are not often hurt when they fight.   Write **Fight**

19. **Swan**   A swan has a long neck.   Write **Swan**
20. **Another**   After trying one, he asked for another.   Write **Another**

19. **True**   It is true that there are seven days in a week.   Write **True**
20. **Dream**   She tried to remember her dream.   Write **Dream**

19. **Hundred**   A hundred is a century.   Write **Hundred**
20. **Ruler**   A ruler is used for measuring.   Write **Ruler**

---

21. **Change**   The cashier gave me the wrong change.   Write **Change**
22. **Marble**   The statue was made from marble.   Write **Marble**

21. **Pencil**   Pencil marks can be rubbed out.   Write **Pencil**
22. **Gentle**   The cat was gentle with the kittens.   Write **Gentle**

21. **Angry**   Angry people sometimes shout.   Write **Angry**
22. **Cattle**   Cattle graze in the fields.   Write **Cattle**

21. **These**   She said, 'I like these better than those.'   Write **These**
22. **Castle**   A castle has thick walls.   Write **Castle**

21. **Orange**   He ate an orange after his dinner.   Write **Orange**
22. **Kettle**   A kettle is for boiling water.   Write **Kettle**

21. **Jungle**   Tigers live in the jungle.   Write **Jungle**
22. **Ticket**   He bought a ticket at the booking office.   Write **Ticket**

---

23. **Picture**   The picture hangs on the wall.   Write **Picture**
24. **Learn**   Sometimes we learn from our mistakes.   Write **Learn**

23. **Notice**   She read the notice.   Write **Notice**
24. **Pretend**   Small children like to pretend.   Write **Pretend**

23. **Promise**   A promise should be kept.   Write **Promise**
24. **Country**   France is a country in Europe.   Write **Country**

23. **Cherry**   A cherry is a small, red fruit.   Write **Cherry**
24. **Build**   We build houses of bricks.   Write **Build**

23. **Worth**   The diamond was worth thousands of pounds.   Write **Worth**
24. **Island**   An island is surrounded by water.   Write **Island**

23. **Dancing**   Dancing is a good way of exercising.   Write **Dancing**
24. **Valley**   A valley lies between hills.   Write **Valley**

# SPELLING TESTS A

25. **Final** The team won its final match of the season. Write **Final**
26. **Argue** They tried to argue politely. Write **Argue**

25. **Square** A square has four sides. Write **Square**
26. **Leather** Leather is used for some shoes. Write **Leather**

25. **Sugar** Sugar makes food sweet. Write **Sugar**
26. **Double** To double a number, multiply by two. Write **Double**

25. **Spare** A car should have a spare tyre. Write **Spare**
26. **Machine** She used a sewing machine to make clothes. Write **Machine**

25. **Hospital** A nurse works in a hospital. Write **Hospital**
26. **Adventure** Most children like adventure stories. Write **Adventure**

25. **Feather** The bird had lost a feather from its wing. Write **Feather**
26. **Knives** Wash the knives and forks. Write **Knives**

27. **Puzzle** A jigsaw puzzle may have hundreds of pieces. Write **Puzzle**
28. **Balance** A tightrope walker has to balance himself. Write **Balance**

27. **Flight** A glider uses rising air for a long flight. Write **Flight**
28. **Repair** He said he could repair my shoes. Write **Repair**

27. **Trousers** In hot climates, men wear short trousers. Write **Trousers**
28. **Thread** To make a necklace, you thread beads on a string. Write **Thread**

27. **Entered** They entered by the front door. Write **Entered**
28. **Scratch** There was a scratch across the paint. Write **Scratch**

27. **Whisper** We whisper when we don't want to be overheard. Write **Whisper**
28. **Kitchen** A cook works in a kitchen. Write **Kitchen**

27. **Scrape** We scrape mud off our shoes. Write **Scrape**
28. **Entrance** The entrance to a cinema is brightly lit. Write **Entrance**

29. **Calm** The sea was calm because there was no wind. Write **Calm**
30. **Question** The question comes before the answer. Write **Question**

29. **Pirate** A pirate was a sea-robber. Write **Pirate**
30. **Dwarf** A dwarf is a very small person. Write **Dwarf**

29. **Lodge** The traveller had to lodge at the inn. Write **Lodge**
30. **Electric** Electric fires are convenient. Write **Electric**

29. **Sword** The soldier carried a sword. Write **Sword**
30. **Passage** He walked down a long passage. Write **Passage**

29. **Wrist** He wore a watch on his wrist. Write **Wrist**
30. **Cabbage** A cabbage is a vegetable. Write **Cabbage**

29. **Damage** Heavy rain can damage crops. Write **Damage**
30. **Judge** The judge passed sentence on the prisoner. Write **Judge**

# SPELLING TESTS A

31. **Quarter** A fourth is a quarter. Write **Quarter**
32. **Heart** The heart pumps blood through our bodies. Write **Heart**

31. **Drawer** Knives and forks are usually kept in a drawer. Write **Drawer**
32. **Industry** Coal-mining was an important industry. Write **Industry**

31. **Whistle** A referee uses a whistle. Write **Whistle**
32. **Careful** Old people are careful on icy pavements. Write **Careful**

31. **Useful** The tools were a useful present. Write **Useful**
32. **Surface** A table has a flat surface. Write **Surface**

31. **Health** Health depends on food and exercise. Write **Health**
32. **Nylon** The rope was made of nylon. Write **Nylon**

31. **Cough** He has a cold and a cough. Write **Cough**
32. **Orchard** They grew apples and pears in the orchard. Write **Orchard**

33. **Crocodile** A crocodile has very large jaws. Write **Crocodile**
34. **Situation** He liked the house but not its situation. Write **Situation**

33. **Saucer** A cup is placed on a saucer. Write **Saucer**
34. **Umbrella** An umbrella provides shelter from the rain. Write **Umbrella**

33. **Biscuit** She had a biscuit with her tea. Write **Biscuit**
34. **Parcel** A parcel should be well wrapped. Write **Parcel**

33. **Label** The label had been scraped off the bottle. Write **Label**
34. **Tortoise** A tortoise is a very slow animal. Write **Tortoise**

33. **Suddenly** It happened so suddenly that they were surprised. Write **Suddenly**
34. **Camera** The photographer put a new film in his camera. Write **Camera**

33. **Cupboard** The plates are in the kitchen cupboard. Write **Cupboard**
34. **Sausage** He enjoys a sausage for breakfast. Write **Sausage**

*End of Year 2 spelling test (34 words)*

35. **Ointment** The ointment helped to heal the cut. Write **Ointment**
36. **Decorate** In December, we decorate the Christmas tree. Write **Decorate**

35. **Bungalow** A bungalow has no upstairs rooms. Write **Bungalow**
36. **Soldier** The soldier fired a gun. Write **Soldier**

35. **Ought** He's late so he ought to hurry. Write **Ought**
36. **Liberty** The prisoner regained his liberty. Write **Liberty**

35. **Photograph** He used his camera to take a photograph. Write **Photograph**
36. **Search** They had to search for the missing climber. Write **Search**

35. **Concert** The band gave a concert last night. Write **Concert**
36. **Favour** He helped me as a favour. Write **Favour**

35. **Flavour** The cake had a chocolate flavour. Write **Flavour**
36. **Meadow** The cows were grazing in the meadow. Write **Meadow**

# SPELLING TESTS A

37. **Several**   Several attempts were made to rescue the climbers.   Write **Several**
38. **Decide**   He couldn't decide what to do.   Write **Decide**

37. **Universal**   The enjoyment of music is universal.   Write **Universal**
38. **Penguin**   A penguin doesn't fly: it swims.   Write **Penguin**

37. **Special**   Most tools have special purposes.   Write **Special**
38. **Enough**   There was enough for everybody.   Write **Enough**

37. **Armour**   Knights were protected by armour.   Write **Armour**
38. **Usual**   The news was broadcast at the usual time.   Write **Usual**

37. **Wander**   He liked to wander off on his own.   Write **Wander**
38. **Invisible**   The stars are invisible during the day.   Write **Invisible**

37. **Chimney**   Smoke rises through a chimney.   Write **Chimney**
38. **Scribble**   Children scribble before they learn to write.   Write **Scribble**

---

39. **Operation**   The operation was successful.   Write **Operation**
40. **Kangaroo**   The kangaroo is an Australian animal.   Write **Kangaroo**

39. **Beauty**   Artists have different ideas about beauty.   Write **Beauty**
40. **Vulture**   A vulture is a large bird of prey.   Write **Vulture**

39. **Headache**   She did not go because she had a headache.   Write **Headache**
40. **Steeple**   A steeple is a tall tower with a spire.   Write **Steeple**

39. **Submarine**   A submarine travels under the sea.   Write **Submarine**
40. **Material**   Nylon is a man-made material.   Write **Material**

39. **Method**   She had a good method for doing the work.   Write **Method**
40. **Cushion**   A cushion is for comfort.   Write **Cushion**

39. **Straight**   The Romans built straight roads.   Write **Straight**
40. **Pleasant**   It is pleasant to walk in the sunshine.   Write **Pleasant**

*End of Year 3 spelling test (40 words)*

---

41. **Cashier**   The cashier took the money to the bank.   Write **Cashier**
42. **Guard**   Alsations are used to guard property.   Write **Guard**

41. **Salute**   The soldier met him with a salute.   Write **Salute**
42. **Impossible**   They said that going to the moon was impossible.   Write **Impossible**

41. **Cathedral**   The service was conducted in the cathedral.   Write **Cathedral**
42. **Assorted**   The bag contained assorted sweets.   Write **Assorted**

41. **Dictionary**   A dictionary lists the meanings of words.   Write **Dictionary**
42. **Honesty**   Honesty is fairness and truthfulness.   Write **Honesty**

41. **Hymn**   Religious services often end with a hymn.   Write **Hymn**
42. **Alteration**   Second thoughts can lead to an alteration.   Write **Alteration**

41. **Terrier**   A terrier is a small dog.   Write **Terrier**
42. **Salmon**   Salmon can leap up waterfalls.   Write **Salmon**

# SPELLING TESTS A

43. **Surprise** An unexpected gift is a pleasant surprise.   Write **Surprise**
44. **Position** He was in a good position to score a goal.   Write **Position**

43. **Mischief** The puppy was full of mischief.   Write **Mischief**
44. **Ordinary** It was an ordinary day: nothing unusual happened.   Write **Ordinary**

43. **Theatre** A theatre puts on plays.   Write **Theatre**
44. **Mystery** The solving of a mystery makes a good story.   Write **Mystery**

43. **Strength** Steel cables have great strength.   Write **Strength**
44. **Probable** When there are black clouds, rain is more probable.   Write **Probable**

43. **Connect** The electrician had to connect the wires.   Write **Connect**
44. **Frightened** The trespassers were frightened by the dog.   Write **Frightened**

43. **Reckon** To reckon is to count or consider.   Write **Reckon**
44. **Lettuce** Lettuce is best when fresh and crisp.   Write **Lettuce**

---

45. **Library** A public library lends books.   Write **Library**
46. **Patient** Customers expect shop assistants to be patient.   Write **Patient**

45. **Ornament** The vase was an attractive ornament.   Write **Ornament**
46. **Examine** He had to examine the car to find the fault.   Write **Examine**

45. **Accident** The fallen tree caused an accident.   Write **Accident**
46. **Approach** The approach to the house was a long drive.   Write **Approach**

45. **Puncture** The puncture in the tyre was caused by a nail.   Write **Puncture**
46. **Disease** We hope to find a cure for every disease.   Write **Disease**

45. **Neither** Neither Jane nor her mother had flown before.   Write **Neither**
46. **Errand** The boy came back from his errand to the shop.   Write **Errand**

45. **Opposite** Black is the opposite of white.   Write **Opposite**
46. **Believe** Some people still believe that the earth is flat.   Write **Believe**

**Table 1:** Tests A Quotients (34 words) – ages 6:4 to 7:11 (Year 2)

| AGE | 6:4 6:5 | 6:6 6:7 | 6:8 6:9 | 6:10 6:11 | 7:0 7:1 | 7:2 7:3 | 7:4 7:5 | 7:6 7:7 | 7:8 7:9 | 7:10 7:11 | AGE |
|---|---|---|---|---|---|---|---|---|---|---|---|
| Score 33 | | >135 | | | | | 134 | 132 | 130 | 128 | Score 33 |
| 32 | | >135 | | | 135 | 132 | 130 | 128 | 126 | 124 | 32 |
| 31 | | | | 135 | 132 | 130 | 127 | 125 | 123 | 121 | 31 |
| 30 | | | 135 | 132 | 129 | 127 | 125 | 123 | 121 | 119 | 30 |
| 29 | | 135 | 132 | 130 | 127 | 125 | 123 | 121 | 119 | 117 | 29 |
| 28 | | 133 | 130 | 128 | 126 | 123 | 121 | 119 | 117 | 116 | 28 |
| 27 | 134 | 131 | 129 | 126 | 124 | 122 | 119 | 117 | 116 | 114 | 27 |
| 26 | 132 | 129 | 127 | 124 | 122 | 120 | 118 | 116 | 114 | 113 | 26 |
| 25 | 130 | 128 | 125 | 123 | 120 | 118 | 116 | 115 | 113 | 111 | 25 |
| 24 | 129 | 126 | 123 | 121 | 119 | 117 | 115 | 113 | 112 | 110 | 24 |
| 23 | 127 | 124 | 122 | 120 | 117 | 115 | 114 | 112 | 110 | 108 | 23 |
| 22 | 125 | 123 | 120 | 118 | 116 | 114 | 112 | 110 | 109 | 107 | 22 |
| 21 | 123 | 121 | 119 | 116 | 114 | 113 | 111 | 109 | 107 | 106 | 21 |
| 20 | 122 | 119 | 117 | 115 | 113 | 111 | 109 | 108 | 106 | 104 | 20 |
| 19 | 120 | 117 | 115 | 113 | 111 | 110 | 108 | 106 | 105 | 103 | 19 |
| 18 | 118 | 116 | 114 | 112 | 110 | 108 | 106 | 105 | 103 | 101 | 18 |
| 17 | 116 | 114 | 112 | 110 | 108 | 107 | 105 | 103 | 101 | 100 | 17 |
| 16 | 114 | 112 | 110 | 109 | 107 | 105 | 103 | 102 | 100 | 98 | 16 |
| 15 | 113 | 111 | 109 | 107 | 105 | 104 | 102 | 100 | 98 | 97 | 15 |
| 14 | 111 | 109 | 107 | 105 | 104 | 102 | 100 | 98 | 97 | 95 | 14 |
| 13 | 109 | 107 | 105 | 104 | 102 | 100 | 98 | 97 | 95 | 94 | 13 |
| 12 | 107 | 106 | 104 | 102 | 100 | 98 | 97 | 95 | 94 | 92 | 12 |
| 11 | 106 | 104 | 102 | 100 | 98 | 97 | 95 | 93 | 92 | 90 | 11 |
| 10 | 104 | 102 | 100 | 98 | 97 | 95 | 93 | 92 | 90 | 89 | 10 |
| 9 | 102 | 100 | 98 | 97 | 95 | 93 | 92 | 90 | 88 | 87 | 9 |
| 8 | 100 | 98 | 96 | 95 | 93 | 91 | 90 | 88 | 87 | 85 | 8 |
| 7 | 98 | 96 | 94 | 93 | 91 | 89 | 88 | 86 | 85 | 84 | 7 |
| 6 | 96 | 94 | 92 | 90 | 89 | 87 | 86 | 84 | 83 | 82 | 6 |
| 5 | 93 | 92 | 90 | 88 | 86 | 85 | 84 | 82 | 81 | 80 | 5 |
| 4 | 91 | 89 | 87 | 86 | 84 | 83 | 82 | 81 | 79 | 78 | 4 |
| 3 | 88 | 86 | 84 | 83 | 82 | 81 | 80 | 78 | 77 | 76 | 3 |
| 2 | 84 | 83 | 81 | 80 | 79 | 78 | 77 | 76 | 75 | 73 | 2 |
| 1 | 79 | 78 | 77 | 77 | 76 | 75 | 74 | 73 | 71 | 70 | 1 |
| AGE | 6:4 6:5 | 6:6 6:7 | 6:8 6:9 | 6:10 6:11 | 7:0 7:1 | 7:2 7:3 | 7:4 7:5 | 7:6 7:7 | 7:8 7:9 | 7:10 7:11 | AGE |

*Table 2:* Tests A Quotients (40 words) – ages 7:0 to 8:11 (Year 3)

| AGE | 7:0 7:1 | 7:2 7:3 | 7:4 7:5 | 7:6 7:7 | 7:8 7:9 | 7:10 7:11 | 8:0 8:1 | 8:2 8:3 | 8:4 8:5 | 8:6 8:7 | 8:8 8:9 | 8:10 8:11 | AGE |
|---|---|---|---|---|---|---|---|---|---|---|---|---|---|
| **Score** | | | | | | | | | | | | | **Score** |
| 39 | | | | | | | 135 | 133 | 131 | 129 | 127 | 125 | 39 |
| 38 | | >135 | | | 134 | 132 | 130 | 128 | 127 | 125 | 123 | 121 | 38 |
| 37 | | | 135 | 133 | 131 | 129 | 127 | 125 | 124 | 122 | 120 | 118 | 37 |
| 36 | | 135 | 133 | 130 | 128 | 126 | 125 | 123 | 121 | 119 | 118 | 116 | 36 |
| 35 | 135 | 133 | 130 | 128 | 126 | 124 | 123 | 121 | 119 | 118 | 116 | 114 | 35 |
| 34 | 133 | 131 | 128 | 126 | 124 | 123 | 121 | 119 | 117 | 116 | 114 | 113 | 34 |
| 33 | 131 | 129 | 127 | 125 | 123 | 121 | 119 | 118 | 116 | 114 | 113 | 111 | 33 |
| 32 | 130 | 127 | 125 | 123 | 121 | 120 | 118 | 116 | 114 | 113 | 111 | 110 | 32 |
| 31 | 128 | 126 | 124 | 122 | 120 | 118 | 116 | 115 | 113 | 111 | 110 | 108 | 31 |
| 30 | 126 | 124 | 122 | 120 | 118 | 117 | 115 | 113 | 112 | 110 | 109 | 107 | 30 |
| 29 | 125 | 123 | 121 | 119 | 117 | 115 | 114 | 112 | 110 | 109 | 107 | 106 | 29 |
| 28 | 124 | 122 | 120 | 118 | 116 | 114 | 113 | 111 | 109 | 108 | 106 | 105 | 28 |
| 27 | 122 | 120 | 118 | 116 | 115 | 113 | 111 | 110 | 108 | 106 | 105 | 104 | 27 |
| 26 | 121 | 119 | 117 | 115 | 113 | 112 | 110 | 108 | 107 | 105 | 104 | 102 | 26 |
| 25 | 119 | 117 | 116 | 114 | 112 | 110 | 109 | 107 | 105 | 104 | 103 | 101 | 25 |
| 24 | 118 | 116 | 114 | 112 | 111 | 109 | 107 | 106 | 104 | 103 | 101 | 100 | 24 |
| 23 | 117 | 115 | 113 | 111 | 109 | 108 | 106 | 104 | 103 | 101 | 100 | 99 | 23 |
| 22 | 115 | 113 | 111 | 110 | 108 | 106 | 105 | 103 | 102 | 100 | 99 | 97 | 22 |
| 21 | 114 | 112 | 110 | 108 | 106 | 105 | 103 | 102 | 100 | 99 | 97 | 96 | 21 |
| 20 | 112 | 110 | 109 | 107 | 105 | 104 | 102 | 100 | 99 | 97 | 96 | 95 | 20 |
| 19 | 111 | 109 | 107 | 105 | 104 | 102 | 101 | 99 | 98 | 96 | 95 | 93 | 19 |
| 18 | 109 | 107 | 106 | 104 | 102 | 101 | 99 | 98 | 96 | 95 | 93 | 92 | 18 |
| 17 | 108 | 106 | 104 | 102 | 101 | 99 | 98 | 96 | 95 | 93 | 92 | 90 | 17 |
| 16 | 106 | 104 | 103 | 101 | 99 | 98 | 96 | 95 | 93 | 92 | 90 | 89 | 16 |
| 15 | 104 | 103 | 101 | 99 | 98 | 96 | 95 | 93 | 92 | 90 | 89 | 87 | 15 |
| 14 | 103 | 101 | 99 | 98 | 96 | 95 | 93 | 92 | 90 | 89 | 87 | 86 | 14 |
| 13 | 101 | 99 | 98 | 96 | 95 | 93 | 92 | 90 | 89 | 87 | 86 | 85 | 13 |
| 12 | 99 | 98 | 96 | 95 | 93 | 92 | 90 | 88 | 87 | 85 | 84 | 83 | 12 |
| 11 | 98 | 96 | 94 | 93 | 91 | 90 | 88 | 87 | 86 | 84 | 83 | 82 | 11 |
| 10 | 96 | 94 | 93 | 91 | 90 | 88 | 87 | 85 | 84 | 83 | 81 | 80 | 10 |
| 9 | 94 | 93 | 91 | 89 | 88 | 86 | 85 | 84 | 82 | 81 | 80 | 79 | 9 |
| 8 | 92 | 91 | 89 | 87 | 86 | 85 | 83 | 82 | 81 | 80 | 79 | 77 | 8 |
| 7 | 90 | 89 | 87 | 86 | 84 | 83 | 82 | 80 | 79 | 78 | 77 | 76 | 7 |
| 6 | 88 | 87 | 85 | 84 | 82 | 81 | 80 | 79 | 78 | 76 | 75 | 74 | 6 |
| 5 | 86 | 85 | 83 | 82 | 81 | 79 | 78 | 77 | 76 | 74 | 73 | 72 | 5 |
| 4 | 84 | 83 | 81 | 80 | 79 | 78 | 76 | 75 | 74 | 72 | 71 | 70 | 4 |
| 3 | 81 | 80 | 79 | 78 | 77 | 75 | 74 | 73 | 71 | 70 | | | 3 |
| 2 | 78 | 77 | 76 | 75 | 74 | 72 | 71 | 70 | | | | | 2 |
| 1 | 75 | 74 | 73 | 72 | 70 | | | | | | <70 | | 1 |
| AGE | 7:0 7:1 | 7:2 7:3 | 7:4 7:5 | 7:6 7:7 | 7:8 7:9 | 7:10 7:11 | 8:0 8:1 | 8:2 8:3 | 8:4 8:5 | 8:6 8:7 | 8:8 8:9 | 8:10 8:11 | AGE |

*Table 3:* Tests A Quotients (46 words) – ages 8:0 to 9:11 (Year 4)

| AGE | 8:0 8:1 | 8:2 8:3 | 8:4 8:5 | 8:6 8:7 | 8:8 8:9 | 8:10 8:11 | 9:0 9:1 | 9:2 9:3 | 9:4 9:5 | 9:6 9:7 | 9:8 9:9 | 9:10 9:11 | AGE |
|---|---|---|---|---|---|---|---|---|---|---|---|---|---|
| Score 45 | | >135 | | | 135 | 134 | 132 | 131 | 130 | 129 | 128 | 127 | Score 45 |
| 44 | | | 135 | 133 | 131 | 130 | 128 | 127 | 125 | 123 | 121 | 120 | 44 |
| 43 | | 134 | 132 | 130 | 128 | 126 | 125 | 123 | 122 | 120 | 118 | 117 | 43 |
| 42 | 133 | 131 | 129 | 127 | 126 | 124 | 122 | 121 | 119 | 117 | 116 | 114 | 42 |
| 41 | 131 | 129 | 127 | 125 | 124 | 122 | 120 | 119 | 117 | 115 | 114 | 113 | 41 |
| 40 | 129 | 127 | 125 | 123 | 122 | 120 | 118 | 117 | 115 | 114 | 112 | 111 | 40 |
| 39 | 127 | 125 | 124 | 122 | 120 | 118 | 117 | 115 | 114 | 112 | 111 | 110 | 39 |
| 38 | 126 | 124 | 122 | 120 | 118 | 117 | 115 | 114 | 112 | 111 | 109 | 108 | 38 |
| 37 | 124 | 122 | 121 | 119 | 117 | 115 | 114 | 112 | 111 | 109 | 108 | 107 | 37 |
| 36 | 123 | 121 | 119 | 117 | 116 | 114 | 113 | 111 | 110 | 108 | 107 | 105 | 36 |
| 35 | 121 | 120 | 118 | 116 | 115 | 113 | 111 | 110 | 108 | 107 | 106 | 104 | 35 |
| 34 | 120 | 118 | 116 | 115 | 113 | 112 | 110 | 109 | 107 | 106 | 104 | 103 | 34 |
| 33 | 119 | 117 | 115 | 114 | 112 | 110 | 109 | 107 | 106 | 105 | 103 | 102 | 33 |
| 32 | 117 | 116 | 114 | 112 | 111 | 109 | 108 | 106 | 105 | 103 | 102 | 101 | 32 |
| 31 | 116 | 114 | 113 | 111 | 109 | 108 | 107 | 105 | 104 | 102 | 101 | 100 | 31 |
| 30 | 115 | 113 | 111 | 110 | 108 | 107 | 105 | 104 | 102 | 101 | 100 | 99 | 30 |
| 29 | 114 | 112 | 110 | 108 | 107 | 106 | 104 | 103 | 101 | 100 | 99 | 98 | 29 |
| 28 | 112 | 111 | 109 | 107 | 106 | 104 | 103 | 102 | 100 | 99 | 98 | 96 | 28 |
| 27 | 111 | 109 | 107 | 106 | 105 | 103 | 102 | 100 | 99 | 98 | 97 | 95 | 27 |
| 26 | 109 | 108 | 106 | 105 | 103 | 102 | 101 | 99 | 98 | 97 | 95 | 94 | 26 |
| 25 | 108 | 106 | 105 | 103 | 102 | 101 | 99 | 98 | 97 | 95 | 94 | 93 | 25 |
| 24 | 107 | 105 | 104 | 102 | 101 | 99 | 98 | 97 | 95 | 94 | 93 | 92 | 24 |
| 23 | 105 | 104 | 102 | 101 | 100 | 98 | 97 | 95 | 94 | 93 | 92 | 90 | 23 |
| 22 | 104 | 103 | 101 | 100 | 98 | 97 | 96 | 94 | 93 | 92 | 90 | 89 | 22 |
| 21 | 103 | 101 | 100 | 98 | 97 | 96 | 94 | 93 | 92 | 90 | 89 | 88 | 21 |
| 20 | 101 | 100 | 99 | 97 | 96 | 94 | 93 | 92 | 90 | 89 | 88 | 87 | 20 |
| 19 | 100 | 99 | 97 | 96 | 94 | 93 | 92 | 90 | 89 | 88 | 87 | 86 | 19 |
| 18 | 99 | 97 | 96 | 94 | 93 | 91 | 90 | 89 | 88 | 87 | 85 | 84 | 18 |
| 17 | 97 | 96 | 94 | 93 | 91 | 90 | 89 | 88 | 86 | 85 | 84 | 83 | 17 |
| 16 | 96 | 94 | 93 | 91 | 90 | 89 | 87 | 86 | 85 | 84 | 83 | 82 | 16 |
| 15 | 94 | 93 | 91 | 90 | 89 | 87 | 86 | 85 | 84 | 83 | 82 | 81 | 15 |
| 14 | 93 | 91 | 90 | 88 | 87 | 86 | 85 | 83 | 82 | 81 | 80 | 79 | 14 |
| 13 | 91 | 90 | 88 | 87 | 86 | 84 | 83 | 82 | 81 | 80 | 79 | 78 | 13 |
| 12 | 90 | 88 | 87 | 85 | 84 | 83 | 82 | 81 | 80 | 79 | 78 | 77 | 12 |
| 11 | 88 | 87 | 85 | 84 | 83 | 82 | 80 | 79 | 78 | 77 | 76 | 75 | 11 |
| 10 | 86 | 85 | 84 | 82 | 81 | 80 | 79 | 78 | 77 | 76 | 75 | 74 | 10 |
| 9 | 85 | 83 | 82 | 81 | 80 | 79 | 78 | 76 | 75 | 74 | 74 | 73 | 9 |
| 8 | 83 | 82 | 81 | 79 | 78 | 77 | 76 | 75 | 74 | 73 | 72 | 71 | 8 |
| 7 | 81 | 80 | 79 | 78 | 77 | 76 | 74 | 73 | 72 | 72 | 71 | 70 | 7 |
| 6 | 80 | 78 | 77 | 76 | 75 | 74 | 73 | 72 | 71 | 70 | | | 6 |
| 5 | 78 | 77 | 76 | 74 | 73 | 72 | 71 | 70 | | | | | 5 |
| 4 | 76 | 75 | 74 | 72 | 71 | 70 | | | | | | | 4 |
| 3 | 74 | 73 | 71 | 70 | | | | <70 | | | | | 3 |
| 2 | 71 | 70 | | | | | | | | | | | 2 |
| AGE | 8:0 8:1 | 8:2 8:3 | 8:4 8:5 | 8:6 8:7 | 8:8 8:9 | 8:10 8:11 | 9:0 9:1 | 9:2 9:3 | 9:4 9:5 | 9:6 9:7 | 9:8 9:9 | 9:10 9:11 | AGE |

## Table 4: Tests A Spelling Ages (in years and tenths)

| Year 2 (34 words) | | Year 3 (40 words) | | Year 4 (46 words) | |
|---|---|---|---|---|---|
| Raw Score | Spelling Age | Raw Score | Spelling Age | Raw Score | Spelling Age |
| <2 | <5.9 | <2 | <5.9 | <2 | <5.9 |
| 2 | 5.9 | 2 | 5.9 | 2 | 5.9 |
| 3 | 6.0 | 3 | 6.0 | 3 | 6.0 |
| 4 | 6.1 | 4 | 6.1 | 4 | 6.1 |
| 5 | 6.2 | 5 | 6.2 | 5 | 6.2 |
| 6 | 6.3 | 6 | 6.3 | 6 | 6.3 |
| 7 | 6.5 | 7 | 6.5 | 7 | 6.5 |
| 8 | 6.6 | 8 | 6.6 | 8 | 6.6 |
| 9 | 6.7 | 9 | 6.7 | 9 | 6.7 |
| 10 | 6.9 | 10 | 6.9 | 10 | 6.9 |
| 11 | 7.0 | 11 | 7.0 | 11 | 7.0 |
| 12 | 7.1 | 12 | 7.1 | 12 | 7.1 |
| 13 | 7.3 | 13 | 7.3 | 13 | 7.3 |
| 14 | 7.4 | 14 | 7.4 | 14 | 7.4 |
| 15 | 7.5 | 15 | 7.5 | 15 | 7.5 |
| 16 | 7.7 | 16 | 7.7 | 16 | 7.7 |
| 17 | 7.8 | 17 | 7.8 | 17 | 7.8 |
| 18 | 8.0 | 18 | 8.0 | 18 | 8.0 |
| 19 | 8.1 | 19 | 8.1 | 19 | 8.1 |
| 20 | 8.2 | 20 | 8.2 | 20 | 8.2 |
| 21 | 8.4 | 21 | 8.4 | 21 | 8.4 |
| 22 | 8.5 | 22 | 8.5 | 22 | 8.5 |
| 23 | 8.6 | 23 | 8.6 | 23 | 8.6 |
| 24 | 8.8 | 24 | 8.8 | 24 | 8.8 |
| 25 | 9.0 | 25 | 9.0 | 25 | 9.0 |
| 26 | 9.1 | 26 | 9.1 | 26 | 9.1 |
| 27 | 9.3 | 27 | 9.3 | 27 | 9.3 |
| 28 | 9.5 | 28 | 9.4 | 28 | 9.4 |
| 29 | 9.7 | 29 | 9.6 | 29 | 9.6 |
| 30 | 9.9 | 30 | 9.8 | 30 | 9.8 |
| 31 | 10.2 | 31 | 10.0 | 31 | 10.0 |
| 32 | 10.5 | 32 | 10.2 | 32 | 10.1 |
| >32 | >11.0 | 33 | 10.4 | 33 | 10.3 |
| | | 34 | 10.6 | 34 | 10.5 |
| | | 35 | 10.8 | 35 | 10.7 |
| | | 36 | 11.1 | 36 | 10.8 |
| | | 37 | 11.4 | 37 | 11.0 |
| | | 38 | 11.9 | 38 | 11.2 |
| | | >38 | >12.5 | 39 | 11.4 |
| | | | | 40 | 11.7 |
| | | | | 41 | 12.0 |
| | | | | 42 | 12.3 |
| | | | | 43 | 12.7 |
| | | | | 44 | 13.2 |
| | | | | >44 | >13.7 |

# SPELLING TESTS B

*Year 5, 44 words.*     *Years 6 and 7, 50 words.*

1. **Tell**   The story he had to tell was interesting.   Write **Tell**
2. **Yet**   The guests haven't arrived yet.   Write **Yet**

1. **Wall**   The bricklayer built a high wall.   Write **Wall**
2. **Jet**   He flew in a jet aeroplane.   Write **Jet**

1. **Pink**   The walls were painted pink.   Write **Pink**
2. **Van**   The furniture was delivered in a van.   Write **Van**

1. **Most**   The blue dress was the most attractive.   Write **Most**
2. **Jug**   She poured the milk into the jug.   Write **Jug**

1. **Tall**   Basketball players are very tall.   Write **Tall**
2. **Tap**   The water dripped from the tap.   Write **Tap**

1. **Egg**   He had an egg for breakfast.   Write **Egg**
2. **With**   We chew with our teeth.   Write **With**

3. **Pond**   There are tadpoles in the pond.   Write **Pond**
4. **Way**   The notice told them which way to go.   Write **Way**

3. **Gold**   Wedding rings are made of gold.   Write **Gold**
4. **Now**   The programme has now begun.   Write **Now**

3. **Open**   He was asked to open the door.   Write **Open**
4. **Trip**   Last summer we went on a day trip.   Write **Trip**

3. **Glad**   He was glad when spring came.   Write **Glad**
4. **Lay**   Hens lay eggs.   Write **Lay**

3. **Time**   A clock measures time.   Write **Time**
4. **How**   The diagram showed how it worked.   Write **How**

3. **That**   He pointed to the one that he wanted.   Write **That**
4. **Hay**   Hay is made from grass.   Write **Hay**

5. **Dish**   The cook put the food in the dish.   Write **Dish**
6. **Mind**   He made up his mind quickly.   Write **Mind**

5. **Snap**   He heard the twig snap.   Write **Snap**
6. **Take**   He had to take the book to the library.   Write **Take**

5. **Gate**   A gate can help to keep a child safe.   Write **Gate**
6. **Plum**   A plum is a fruit with a large stone.   Write **Plum**

5. **Gave**   He gave his bus fare to the driver.   Write **Gave**
6. **Head**   She took the hat off her head.   Write **Head**

5. **Pram**   A pram has a brake for safety.   Write **Pram**
6. **Rush**   You will have to rush to catch the bus.   Write **Rush**

5. **Year**   He was fifteen last year.   Write **Year**
6. **Shut**   She was asked to shut the door.   Write **Shut**

# SPELLING TESTS B

7. **Pack** The hiker had a pack on his back. Write **Pack**
8. **Desk** He was writing at his desk. Write **Desk**

7. **Moth** A moth is an insect. Write **Moth**
8. **Each** Each person was given an apple. Write **Each**

7. **Sack** The post was delivered in a sack. Write **Sack**
8. **Nail** Each finger has a nail. Write **Nail**

7. **Gift** The bicycle was a birthday gift. Write **Gift**
8. **Yard** He kept his bike in the yard. Write **Yard**

7. **Bird** A bird sings. Write **Bird**
8. **Skin** A frog has cold skin. Write **Skin**

7. **Page** He opened the book at the first page. Write **Page**
8. **Fact** It is a fact that the sun rose this morning. Write **Fact**

---

9. **Stick** The old man carried a walking stick. Write **Stick**
10. **Puppy** A puppy is a young dog. Write **Puppy**

9. **Strong** Samson was a strong man. Write **Strong**
10. **Horse** A horse is kept in a stable. Write **Horse**

9. **Mouse** The cat chased the mouse. Write **Mouse**
10. **Plenty** In the summer, birds have plenty to eat. Write **Plenty**

9. **Shave** Men have to shave every morning. Write **Shave**
10. **Gone** The visitors have gone home. Write **Gone**

9. **Table** We eat at a table. Write **Table**
10. **Only** He was only three years old. Write **Only**

9. **Mine** The bicycle wasn't mine. Write **Mine**
10. **Soap** We used soap to wash ourselves. Write **Soap**

---

11. **Ladder** A window cleaner uses a ladder. Write **Ladder**
12. **Pound** There are one hundred pence in a pound. Write **Pound**

11. **Brother** Peter has a brother called John. Write **Brother**
12. **Amount** The cashier knew it was the correct amount. Write **Amount**

11. **Cloudy** Cloudy weather often brings rain. Write **Cloudy**
12. **Charge** There was no charge for admission. Write **Charge**

11. **Thunder** Thunder comes after lightning. Write **Thunder**
12. **Chase** There was a chase and the robber was caught. Write **Chase**

11. **Cleaner** After its bath, the dog looked cleaner. Write **Cleaner**
12. **Caravan** During the holiday he lived in a caravan. Write **Caravan**

11. **Slipper** When I broke my toe I had to wear a slipper. Write **Slipper**
12. **Sound** He didn't like the sound of the engine. Write **Sound**

# SPELLING TESTS B

13. **Artist**  The artist was painting a picture.  Write **Artist**
14. **Early**  The early bird catches the worm.  Write **Early**

13. **Narrow**  The road was too narrow for a lorry.  Write **Narrow**
14. **Quick**  If you are quick you will catch the bus.  Write **Quick**

13. **Shadow**  At sunset the tower cast a long shadow.  Write **Shadow**
14. **Ginger**  The shop sold ginger biscuits.  Write **Ginger**

13. **Reach**  The shelf was just out of reach.  Write **Reach**
14. **Pillow**  The tramp used his coat for a pillow.  Write **Pillow**

13. **Mistake**  He corrected his mistake.  Write **Mistake**
14. **Sparrow**  A sparrow is a small bird.  Write **Sparrow**

13. **Spread**  Oak trees spread their branches a long way.  Write **Spread**
14. **Branch**  The wind broke the branch off the tree.  Write **Branch**

15. **Towel**  Dry your hands on the towel.  Write **Towel**
16. **Always**  An elephant always has a trunk.  Write **Always**

15. **Shampoo**  Shampoo is for washing hair.  Write **Shampoo**
16. **Crowd**  A crowd is a gathering of people.  Write **Crowd**

15. **Wrong**  The motorist was directed the wrong way.  Write **Wrong**
16. **Frozen**  Many people buy frozen foods.  Write **Frozen**

15. **Husband**  The woman's husband paid the bill.  Write **Husband**
16. **Holiday**  They had a walking holiday.  Write **Holiday**

15. **Blanket**  The baby was wrapped in a blanket.  Write **Blanket**
16. **Noise**  The noise of the engine was deafening.  Write **Noise**

15. **Worst**  The last game produced their worst result.  Write **Worst**
16. **Swimming**  He went to the pool for his swimming lesson.  Write **Swimming**

17. **Bubble**  He watched the bubble rising in the water.  Write **Bubble**
18. **Butcher**  The butcher sells meat.  Write **Butcher**

17. **Beard**  The man shaved off his beard.  Write **Beard**
18. **Tumble**  Clowns tumble about to make people laugh.  Write **Tumble**

17. **Fetch**  Fetch the newspaper.  Write **Fetch**
18. **Lemonade**  Cold lemonade is a drink for a hot day.  Write **Lemonade**

17. **Hungry**  If you miss a meal you become hungry.  Write **Hungry**
18. **Strange**  A strange noise was coming from the engine.  Write **Strange**

17. **Office**  Most secretaries work in an office.  Write **Office**
18. **Afraid**  The mouse was afraid of the cat.  Write **Afraid**

17. **Ribbon**  Ribbon is sometimes used to decorate hats.  Write **Ribbon**
18. **Grumble**  He had no need to grumble.  Write **Grumble**

# SPELLING TESTS B

19. **Comb**   A comb is used to keep hair tidy.   Write **Comb**
20. **Mountain**   They went to climb the mountain.   Write **Mountain**

19. **Juice**   She drinks orange juice.   Write **Juice**
20. **Manage**   He could just manage to lift the box by himself.   Write **Manage**

19. **Bomb**   The bomb exploded.   Write **Bomb**
20. **Hedge**   He planted a garden hedge.   Write **Hedge**

19. **Badge**   He had a badge pinned to his jacket.   Write **Badge**
20. **Crumb**   Not a crumb of bread was left.   Write **Crumb**

19. **Climb**   They trained to climb the mountain.   Write **Climb**
20. **Bandage**   He found a bandage in the first-aid box.   Write **Bandage**

19. **Village**   The village was two miles away.   Write **Village**
20. **Jockey**   The jockey fell off the horse.   Write **Jockey**

---

21. **Register**   A register is a list of names.   Write **Register**
22. **Thirsty**   We drink when we are thirsty.   Write **Thirsty**

21. **Important**   Clear writing is important for readers.   Write **Important**
22. **Plough**   We plough the fields before sowing the seed.   Write **Plough**

21. **Shoulder**   He carried the ladder on his shoulder.   Write **Shoulder**
22. **Curtain**   A curtain at the window keeps a room private.   Write **Curtain**

21. **Station**   The train arrived at the station.   Write **Station**
22. **Ambulance**   The ambulance takes people to hospital.   Write **Ambulance**

21. **Capture**   You need a licence to capture deer.   Write **Capture**
22. **Chemist**   A chemist studies how substances are made.   Write **Chemist**

21. **Action**   The goalkeeper's action was clumsy.   Write **Action**
22. **Terrible**   The earthquake was a terrible disaster.   Write **Terrible**

---

23. **Telescope**   The telescope enables us to see great distances.   Write **Telescope**
24. **Harbour**   A harbour is a safe place for ships.   Write **Harbour**

23. **Magazine**   A magazine has to interest its readers.   Write **Magazine**
24. **Violet**   A violet grows well in the shade.   Write **Violet**

23. **Figure**   He saw a tall dark figure in the fog.   Write **Figure**
24. **Lightning**   Lightning comes before thunder.   Write **Lightning**

23. **Television**   Television sets can be bought or rented.   Write **Television**
24. **Furniture**   Furniture makes life more comfortable.   Write **Furniture**

23. **Treasure**   There are many stories about looking for treasure.   Write **Treasure**
24. **Avenue**   An avenue has trees along it.   Write **Avenue**

23. **Marmalade**   Marmalade is usually made from oranges.   Write **Marmalade**
24. **Coloured**   The dye coloured her clothes.   Write **Coloured**

# SPELLING TESTS B

25. **Fault**  The electrician found the fault.  Write **Fault**
26. **Personal**  Some newspapers print personal messages.  Write **Personal**

25. **Tough**  The skin of an elephant is tough.  Write **Tough**
26. **Cucumber**  Cucumber is used in salads.  Write **Cucumber**

25. **Producer**  The success of a play depends on its producer.  Write **Producer**
26. **Guitar**  A guitar usually has six strings.  Write **Guitar**

25. **Conductor**  A conductor guides an orchestra.  Write **Conductor**
26. **General**  The general commanded the tank force.  Write **General**

25. **Passenger**  The bus had room for one more passenger.  Write **Passenger**
26. **Razor**  A razor is for shaving.  Write **Razor**

25. **Difference**  The difference between four and six is two.  Write **Difference**
26. **Radiator**  The radiator made the room warm.  Write **Radiator**

---

27. **Umpire**  The umpire said the player was out.  Write **Umpire**
28. **Suppose**  I suppose she lost her gloves while shopping.  Write **Suppose**

27. **Pigeon**  A pigeon is a racing bird.  Write **Pigeon**
28. **Laundry**  A laundry is a place for washing clothes.  Write **Laundry**

27. **Practical**  Good cooks are practical people.  Write **Practical**
28. **Aeroplane**  Travelling by aeroplane is quicker.  Write **Aeroplane**

27. **Taught**  He taught his son to play cricket.  Write **Taught**
28. **Margarine**  Butter and margarine are eaten on bread.  Write **Margarine**

27. **Stitch**  She had to stitch the buttons on.  Write **Stitch**
28. **Parachute**  The parachute saved the pilot's life.  Write **Parachute**

27. **Microphone**  A broadcaster uses a microphone.  Write **Microphone**
28. **Autumn**  Autumn follows summer.  Write **Autumn**

---

29. **Skeleton**  In the museum there was the skeleton of a dinosaur.  Write **Skeleton**
30. **Exercise**  Physical exercise keeps people healthy.  Write **Exercise**

29. **Fierce**  Animals can be fierce about food.  Write **Fierce**
30. **Giraffe**  A giraffe has a long neck.  Write **Giraffe**

27. **Shepherd**  The shepherd is very busy in the spring.  Write **Shepherd**
30. **Stomach**  Food is digested in the stomach.  Write **Stomach**

27. **Squirrel**  The squirrel stores food for the winter.  Write **Squirrel**
30. **Ventilation**  Doors, windows and chimneys provide ventilation.  Write **Ventilation**

27. **Instruction**  They followed each instruction with care.  Write **Instruction**
30. **Deserve**  The athletes have trained hard and deserve to win.  Write **Deserve**

27. **Celebration**  A celebration is to mark a special occasion.  Write **Celebration**
30. **Quarrel**  To quarrel is unpleasant.  Write **Quarrel**

# SPELLING TESTS B

31. **Programme**  They watched the television sports programme.  Write **Programme**
32. **Calendar**  A calendar shows the months and days.  Write **Calendar**

31. **Vinegar**  Onions are sometimes kept in vinegar.  Write **Vinegar**
32. **Surrender**  The defeated army had to surrender.  Write **Surrender**

31. **Anchor**  An anchor prevents a boat from drifting.  Write **Anchor**
32. **Article**  Each article had its own label.  Write **Article**

31. **Squeeze**  You squeeze a sponge to remove the water.  Write **Squeeze**
32. **Burglar**  Many shops are fitted with burglar alarms.  Write **Burglar**

31. **Circular**  One tin was square, the other was circular.  Write **Circular**
32. **Knuckle**  A bruised knuckle can be very painful.  Write **Knuckle**

31. **Wrestle**  Young gorillas like to wrestle.  Write **Wrestle**
32. **Equator**  It is hot near the equator.  Write **Equator**

---

33. **Tongue**  His mouth and tongue were dry.  Write **Tongue**
34. **Scientific**  The expedition has scientific work to do.  Write **Scientific**

33. **Separate**  To make butter you separate cream from milk.  Write **Separate**
34. **Yacht**  A racing yacht has huge sails.  Write **Yacht**

33. **Gracious**  The woman had gracious manners.  Write **Gracious**
34. **Bicycle**  You can easily fall off a bicycle.  Write **Bicycle**

33. **Scissors**  Scissors should be kept sharp.  Write **Scissors**
34. **Reindeer**  Herds of reindeer can be found in Greenland.  Write **Reindeer**

33. **Unfortunate**  The jockey had an unfortunate day.  Write **Unfortunate**
34. **Knowledge**  Encyclopedias contain our knowledge of the world.  Write **Knowledge**

33. **Punctual**  All the guests were punctual.  Write **Punctual**
34  **Neighbour**  Her neighbour helps to cut the hedge. Write **Neighbour**

---

35. **Crystal**  A rock may contain many kinds of crystal.  Write **Crystal**
36. **Distinguish**  They could not distinguish between friend and foe.  Write **Distinguish**

35. **Vegetable**  A cabbage is a vegetable.  Write **Vegetable**
36. **Satisfy**  There was enough food to satisfy everyone.  Write **Satisfy**

35. **Miserable**  Holidays can be made miserable by bad weather.  Write **Miserable**
36. **Engineer**  The ship's captain relies on his engineer.  Write **Engineer**

35. **Extinguish**  The firemen tried to extinguish the fire.  Write **Extinguish**
36. **Valuable**  Even small diamonds are valuable.  Write **Valuable**

35. **Envelope**  The letter came in a large envelope.  Write **Envelope**
36. **Responsible**  If you are responsible you take the blame and the credit.  Write **Responsible**

35. **Impatient**  He was impatient because he was in a hurry.  Write **Impatient**
36. **Expression**  His expression revealed his feelings.  Write **Expression**

# SPELLING TESTS B

37. **University**  A university is for teaching and research.  Write **University**
38. **Particular**  It was a matter of particular importance.  Write **Particular**

37. **Handkerchief**  A handkerchief can be made of cotton or paper.  Write **Handkerchief**
38. **Obstinate**  It is said that mules are obstinate.  Write **Obstinate**

37. **Carriage**  There were seats in the last carriage of the train.  Write **Carriage**
38. **Atmosphere**  Oxygen is one of the gases in the atmosphere.  Write **Atmosphere**

37. **Favourite**  Most people have a favourite TV programme.  Write **Favourite**
38. **Disappear**  The magician made things disappear.  Write **Disappear**

37. **Sheriff**  A sheriff is an officer of the law.  Write **Sheriff**
38. **Experience**  Walking on the moon is a very rare experience.  Write **Experience**

37. **Coronation**  The king's coronation was shown on television.  Write **Coronation**
38. **Queue**  A queue enables people to be dealt with fairly.  Write **Queue**

---

39. **Society**  Every society has different customs.  Write **Society**
40. **Spectacle**  The ceremony was a memorable spectacle.  Write **Spectacle**

39. **Audience**  The audience applauded the speaker.  Write **Audience**
40. **Physical**  Fresh air and physical exercise are healthy.  Write **Physical**

39. **Icicle**  The water from the snow formed an icicle.  Write **Icicle**
40. **Furnace**  Steel is produced in a furnace.  Write **Furnace**

39. **Cauliflower**  Cauliflower is a vegetable.  Write **Cauliflower**
40. **Official**  There was an official announcement.  Write **Official**

39. **Exhaust**  An exhaust pipe carries the gases from the engine.  Write **Exhaust**
40. **Mechanical**  Electronic games are replacing mechanical toys.  Write **Mechanical**

39. **Cylinder**  The carpet arrived rolled up in a cylinder.  Write **Cylinder**
40. **Vehicle**  A vehicle is for carrying people or objects.  Write **Vehicle**

---

41. **Foreign**  It is useful to know a foreign language.  Write **Foreign**
42. **Collapse**  The heat caused some runners to collapse.  Write **Collapse**

41. **Aquarium**  The fish in the aquarium need expert attention.  Write **Aquarium**
42. **Rumour**  Rumour is often untrue.  Write **Rumour**

41. **Hyena**  A hyena looks like a dog.  Write **Hyena**
42. **Dynamite**  Dynamite is used in quarries.  Write **Dynamite**

41. **Rhymes**  'Bread' rhymes with 'head'.  Write **Rhymes**
42. **Propeller**  A motor boat has a propeller.  Write **Propeller**

41. **Turpentine**  Turpentine is used by house painters.  Write **Turpentine**
42. **Leisure**  He enjoyed his leisure time.  Write **Leisure**

41. **Character**  The actor did not like playing that character.  Write **Character**
42. **Behaviour**  He studies the behaviour of animals.  Write **Behaviour**

# SPELLING TESTS B

43. Association   He joined a professional association.   Write **Association**
44. Accomplish   They had to accomplish the work quickly.   Write **Accomplish**

43. Procession   A procession has to go along a planned route.   Write **Procession**
44. Appetite   The fresh air and exercise gave him an appetite.   Write **Appetite**

43. Expedition   The expedition was successful.   Write **Expedition**
44. Ridiculous   The man looked ridiculous on the donkey.   Write **Ridiculous**

43. Precious   Platinum is a precious metal.   Write **Precious**
44. Inferior   The inferior foods couldn't be sold.   Write **Inferior**

43. Exterior   The exterior of the house needs painting.   Write **Exterior**
44. Delicious   The fresh fruit tasted delicious.   Write **Delicious**

43. Ingenious   The new gadget was ingenious.   Write **Ingenious**
44. Illumination   Candles provide very poor illumination.   Write **Illumination**

*End of Year 5 spelling test (44 words)*

45. Apparatus   Apparatus is tools, equipment, machines, etc.   Write **Apparatus**
46. Ceremony   The ceremony lasted all day.   Write **Ceremony**

45. Introductory   The discussion followed an introductory talk.   Write **Introductory**
46. Moustache   The man had a moustache and a beard.   Write **Moustache**

45. Appreciate   Some people do not appreciate music.   Write **Appreciate**
46. Thorough   The work was thorough and the result was good.   Write **Thorough**

45. Secretary   The secretary typed the letters.   Write **Secretary**
46. Fatigue   Fatigue made it difficult to continue.   Write **Fatigue**

45. Anniversary   There was a party to celebrate the anniversary.   Write **Anniversary**
46. Nuisance   Dogs that bark all the time are a nuisance.   Write **Nuisance**

45. Parliament   Many countries have a parliament.   Write **Parliament**
46. Hippopotamus   A hippopotamus lives in a pool or river.   Write **Hippopotamus**

47. Refrigerator   A refrigerator keeps food cool and fresh.   Write **Refrigerator**
48. Efficient   The machine was efficient.   Write **Efficient**

47. Paraffin   Paraffin was once used for lighting houses.   Write **Paraffin**
48. Immediately   He knocked, and the door was opened immediately.   Write **Immediately**

47. Peculiar   She disliked its peculiar flavour.   Write **Peculiar**
48. Somersault   To somersault is to turn heels over head.   Write **Somersault**

47. Catalogue   The company's products appeared in the catalogue.   Write **Catalogue**
48. Sufficient   The food supply was sufficient for the voyage.   Write **Sufficient**

47. Diesel   Most lorries have diesel engines.   Write **Diesel**
48. Conspicuous   The very tall man was conspicuous in the crowd.   Write **Conspicuous**

47. Fugitive   The fugitive hid from his pursuers.   Write **Fugitive**
48. Receive   She likes to receive letters.   Write **Receive**

# SPELLING TESTS B

49. **Condemn**   The safety inspector had to condemn the building.   Write **Condemn**
50. **Prophecy**   The prophecy did not come true.   Write **Prophecy**

49. **Interrupt**   Announcers sometimes interrupt programmes with news.   Write **Interrupt**
50. **Conscious**   He wasn't conscious of what was happening.   Write **Conscious**

49. **Aerial**   In some areas, a good TV aerial is essential.   Write **Aerial**
50. **Committee**   The committee met and decided what to do.   Write **Committee**

49. **Dormitory**   A dormitory is a room where many people sleep.   Write **Dormitory**
50. **Persevere**   He had to persevere in order to win.   Write **Persevere**

49. **Necessary**   Repairing the road was necessary.   Write **Necessary**
50. **Conscience**   His crimes troubled his conscience.   Write **Conscience**

49. **Sergeant**   The soldiers were drilled by their sergeant.   Write **Sergeant**
50. **Solemn**   The listened to the judge in solemn silence.   Write **Solemn**

*Table 5:* Tests B Quotients (44 words) – ages 9:0 to 10:11 (Year 5)

| AGE | 9:0/9:1 | 9:2/9:3 | 9:4/9:5 | 9:6/9:7 | 9:8/9:9 | 9:10/9:11 | 10:0/10:1 | 10:2/10:3 | 10:4/10:5 | 10:6/10:7 | 10:8/10:9 | 10:10/10:11 | AGE |
|---|---|---|---|---|---|---|---|---|---|---|---|---|---|
| Score 43 |  |  | >135 |  |  |  |  |  |  | 135 | 133 | 132 | Score 43 |
| 42 |  |  |  |  |  |  | 135 | 134 | 132 | 130 | 129 | 127 | 42 |
| 41 |  |  |  |  | 135 | 134 | 132 | 130 | 128 | 127 | 125 | 124 | 41 |
| 40 |  |  | 135 | 134 | 132 | 130 | 129 | 127 | 125 | 124 | 122 | 121 | 40 |
| 39 |  | 135 | 133 | 131 | 130 | 128 | 126 | 124 | 123 | 122 | 120 | 119 | 39 |
| 38 | 134 | 132 | 130 | 129 | 127 | 126 | 124 | 122 | 121 | 119 | 118 | 117 | 38 |
| 37 | 132 | 130 | 128 | 127 | 125 | 124 | 122 | 120 | 119 | 118 | 116 | 115 | 37 |
| 36 | 130 | 128 | 127 | 125 | 123 | 122 | 120 | 119 | 117 | 116 | 115 | 113 | 36 |
| 35 | 128 | 126 | 125 | 123 | 122 | 120 | 118 | 117 | 116 | 115 | 113 | 112 | 35 |
| 34 | 126 | 125 | 123 | 121 | 120 | 118 | 117 | 115 | 114 | 113 | 112 | 111 | 34 |
| 33 | 125 | 123 | 121 | 120 | 118 | 117 | 115 | 114 | 113 | 112 | 111 | 109 | 33 |
| 32 | 123 | 121 | 120 | 118 | 117 | 115 | 114 | 113 | 112 | 110 | 109 | 108 | 32 |
| 31 | 122 | 120 | 118 | 117 | 115 | 114 | 113 | 112 | 110 | 109 | 108 | 107 | 31 |
| 30 | 120 | 118 | 117 | 115 | 114 | 113 | 111 | 110 | 109 | 108 | 107 | 105 | 30 |
| 29 | 118 | 117 | 115 | 114 | 113 | 111 | 110 | 109 | 108 | 107 | 105 | 104 | 29 |
| 28 | 117 | 115 | 114 | 113 | 111 | 110 | 109 | 108 | 106 | 105 | 104 | 103 | 28 |
| 27 | 115 | 114 | 112 | 111 | 110 | 109 | 107 | 106 | 105 | 104 | 103 | 102 | 27 |
| 26 | 114 | 112 | 111 | 110 | 109 | 107 | 106 | 105 | 104 | 103 | 101 | 100 | 26 |
| 25 | 112 | 111 | 110 | 109 | 107 | 106 | 105 | 104 | 102 | 101 | 100 | 99 | 25 |
| 24 | 111 | 110 | 108 | 107 | 106 | 105 | 103 | 102 | 101 | 100 | 99 | 98 | 24 |
| 23 | 110 | 108 | 107 | 106 | 105 | 103 | 102 | 101 | 100 | 99 | 98 | 97 | 23 |
| 22 | 108 | 107 | 106 | 105 | 103 | 102 | 101 | 100 | 99 | 98 | 97 | 96 | 22 |
| 21 | 107 | 106 | 104 | 103 | 102 | 101 | 100 | 98 | 97 | 96 | 95 | 94 | 21 |
| 20 | 105 | 104 | 103 | 102 | 101 | 99 | 98 | 97 | 96 | 95 | 94 | 93 | 20 |
| 19 | 104 | 103 | 102 | 100 | 99 | 98 | 97 | 96 | 95 | 94 | 93 | 92 | 19 |
| 18 | 103 | 101 | 100 | 99 | 98 | 97 | 96 | 95 | 94 | 93 | 92 | 91 | 18 |
| 17 | 101 | 100 | 99 | 98 | 97 | 96 | 94 | 93 | 92 | 91 | 90 | 89 | 17 |
| 16 | 100 | 99 | 98 | 96 | 95 | 94 | 93 | 92 | 91 | 90 | 89 | 88 | 16 |
| 15 | 99 | 97 | 96 | 95 | 94 | 93 | 92 | 91 | 90 | 89 | 88 | 87 | 15 |
| 14 | 97 | 96 | 95 | 94 | 93 | 92 | 90 | 89 | 88 | 87 | 86 | 86 | 14 |
| 13 | 96 | 95 | 94 | 92 | 91 | 90 | 89 | 88 | 87 | 86 | 85 | 84 | 13 |
| 12 | 95 | 93 | 92 | 91 | 90 | 89 | 88 | 87 | 86 | 85 | 84 | 83 | 12 |
| 11 | 93 | 92 | 91 | 90 | 88 | 87 | 86 | 85 | 85 | 84 | 83 | 82 | 11 |
| 10 | 92 | 90 | 89 | 88 | 87 | 86 | 85 | 84 | 83 | 82 | 81 | 81 | 10 |
| 9 | 90 | 89 | 88 | 87 | 86 | 85 | 84 | 83 | 82 | 81 | 80 | 79 | 9 |
| 8 | 89 | 88 | 86 | 85 | 84 | 83 | 82 | 81 | 81 | 80 | 79 | 78 | 8 |
| 7 | 87 | 86 | 85 | 84 | 83 | 82 | 81 | 80 | 79 | 78 | 78 | 77 | 7 |
| 6 | 86 | 84 | 83 | 82 | 81 | 80 | 79 | 79 | 78 | 77 | 76 | 75 | 6 |
| 5 | 84 | 83 | 82 | 81 | 80 | 79 | 78 | 77 | 76 | 76 | 75 | 74 | 5 |
| 4 | 82 | 81 | 80 | 79 | 78 | 77 | 77 | 76 | 75 | 74 | 73 | 72 | 4 |
| 3 | 80 | 79 | 78 | 77 | 76 | 76 | 75 | 74 | 73 | 72 | 71 | 71 | 3 |
| 2 | 78 | 77 | 76 | 75 | 75 | 74 | 73 | 72 | 71 | 70 |  |  | 2 |
| 1 | 75 | 74 | 73 | 73 | 72 | 71 | 70 | 70 |  |  | <70 |  | 1 |

*Table 6:* Tests B Quotients (50 words) – ages 10:0 to 12:11 (Years 6 and 7)

| AGE | 10:0 10:1 | 10:2 10:3 | 10:4 10:5 | 10:6 10:7 | 10:8 10:9 | 10:10 10:11 | 11:0 11:1 | 11:2 11:3 | 11:4 11:5 | 11:6 11:7 | 11:8 11:9 | 11:10 11:11 | 12:0 12:1 | 12:2 12:3 | 12:4 12:5 | 12:6 12:7 | 12:8 12:9 | 12:10 12:11 | AGE |
|---|---|---|---|---|---|---|---|---|---|---|---|---|---|---|---|---|---|---|---|
| Score | | | | | | | | | | | | | | | | | | | Score |
| 49 | | <135 | | | | | | 135 | 133 | 132 | 131 | 129 | 128 | 127 | 126 | 125 | 124 | 123 | 49 |
| 48 | | | | | | 134 | 133 | 131 | 130 | 129 | 127 | 126 | 125 | 124 | 123 | 122 | 121 | 120 | 48 |
| 47 | | | | 135 | 133 | 131 | 130 | 128 | 127 | 126 | 124 | 123 | 122 | 121 | 120 | 119 | 118 | 117 | 47 |
| 46 | | | 134 | 132 | 130 | 129 | 127 | 126 | 125 | 123 | 122 | 121 | 120 | 119 | 118 | 117 | 116 | 115 | 46 |
| 45 | 135 | 133 | 131 | 130 | 128 | 127 | 125 | 124 | 123 | 121 | 120 | 119 | 118 | 117 | 116 | 115 | 114 | 113 | 45 |
| 44 | 132 | 131 | 129 | 127 | 126 | 125 | 123 | 122 | 121 | 119 | 118 | 117 | 116 | 115 | 114 | 113 | 112 | 111 | 44 |
| 43 | 130 | 129 | 127 | 125 | 124 | 123 | 121 | 120 | 119 | 117 | 116 | 115 | 114 | 113 | 112 | 111 | 110 | 109 | 43 |
| 42 | 128 | 127 | 125 | 124 | 122 | 121 | 120 | 118 | 117 | 116 | 115 | 113 | 112 | 111 | 110 | 109 | 108 | 108 | 42 |
| 41 | 126 | 125 | 123 | 122 | 120 | 119 | 118 | 117 | 116 | 114 | 113 | 112 | 111 | 110 | 109 | 108 | 107 | 106 | 41 |
| 40 | 124 | 123 | 122 | 120 | 119 | 118 | 116 | 115 | 114 | 113 | 112 | 111 | 109 | 108 | 107 | 106 | 106 | 105 | 40 |
| 39 | 123 | 121 | 120 | 119 | 118 | 116 | 115 | 114 | 113 | 111 | 110 | 109 | 108 | 107 | 106 | 105 | 104 | 104 | 39 |
| 38 | 121 | 120 | 119 | 117 | 116 | 115 | 114 | 112 | 111 | 110 | 109 | 108 | 107 | 106 | 105 | 104 | 103 | 102 | 38 |
| 37 | 120 | 119 | 117 | 116 | 115 | 114 | 112 | 111 | 110 | 109 | 108 | 107 | 105 | 104 | 103 | 103 | 102 | 101 | 37 |
| 36 | 118 | 117 | 116 | 115 | 113 | 112 | 111 | 110 | 109 | 108 | 106 | 105 | 104 | 103 | 102 | 102 | 101 | 100 | 36 |
| 35 | 117 | 116 | 115 | 113 | 112 | 111 | 110 | 109 | 107 | 106 | 105 | 104 | 103 | 102 | 101 | 100 | 100 | 99 | 35 |
| 34 | 116 | 115 | 113 | 112 | 111 | 110 | 108 | 107 | 106 | 105 | 104 | 103 | 102 | 101 | 100 | 99 | 99 | 98 | 34 |
| 33 | 114 | 113 | 112 | 111 | 110 | 108 | 107 | 106 | 105 | 104 | 103 | 102 | 101 | 100 | 99 | 98 | 97 | 97 | 33 |
| 32 | 113 | 112 | 111 | 109 | 108 | 107 | 106 | 105 | 104 | 103 | 102 | 101 | 100 | 99 | 98 | 97 | 96 | 96 | 32 |
| 31 | 112 | 111 | 109 | 108 | 107 | 106 | 105 | 103 | 102 | 101 | 100 | 99 | 98 | 98 | 97 | 96 | 95 | 94 | 31 |
| 30 | 111 | 109 | 108 | 107 | 106 | 105 | 103 | 102 | 101 | 100 | 99 | 98 | 97 | 96 | 96 | 95 | 94 | 93 | 30 |
| 29 | 109 | 108 | 107 | 106 | 104 | 103 | 102 | 101 | 100 | 99 | 98 | 97 | 96 | 95 | 94 | 94 | 93 | 92 | 29 |
| 28 | 108 | 107 | 105 | 104 | 103 | 102 | 101 | 100 | 99 | 98 | 97 | 96 | 95 | 94 | 93 | 93 | 92 | 91 | 28 |
| 27 | 106 | 105 | 104 | 103 | 102 | 101 | 100 | 99 | 98 | 97 | 96 | 95 | 94 | 93 | 92 | 91 | 91 | 90 | 27 |
| 26 | 105 | 104 | 103 | 102 | 101 | 100 | 99 | 98 | 97 | 96 | 95 | 94 | 93 | 92 | 91 | 90 | 90 | 89 | 26 |
| 25 | 104 | 103 | 102 | 101 | 99 | 98 | 97 | 96 | 95 | 94 | 93 | 93 | 92 | 91 | 90 | 89 | 89 | 88 | 25 |
| 24 | 103 | 101 | 100 | 99 | 98 | 97 | 96 | 95 | 94 | 93 | 92 | 91 | 91 | 90 | 89 | 88 | 87 | 87 | 24 |
| 23 | 101 | 100 | 99 | 98 | 97 | 96 | 95 | 94 | 93 | 92 | 91 | 90 | 89 | 89 | 88 | 87 | 86 | 86 | 23 |
| 22 | 100 | 99 | 98 | 97 | 96 | 95 | 94 | 93 | 92 | 91 | 90 | 89 | 88 | 87 | 87 | 86 | 85 | 85 | 22 |
| 21 | 99 | 98 | 97 | 96 | 95 | 94 | 93 | 92 | 91 | 90 | 89 | 88 | 87 | 86 | 86 | 85 | 84 | 84 | 21 |
| 20 | 98 | 97 | 95 | 94 | 93 | 92 | 91 | 90 | 90 | 89 | 88 | 87 | 86 | 85 | 85 | 84 | 83 | 83 | 20 |
| 19 | 96 | 95 | 94 | 93 | 92 | 91 | 90 | 89 | 88 | 87 | 87 | 86 | 85 | 84 | 84 | 83 | 82 | 82 | 19 |
| 18 | 95 | 94 | 93 | 92 | 91 | 90 | 89 | 88 | 87 | 86 | 86 | 85 | 84 | 83 | 83 | 82 | 81 | 81 | 18 |
| 17 | 94 | 93 | 92 | 91 | 90 | 89 | 88 | 87 | 86 | 85 | 84 | 84 | 83 | 82 | 81 | 81 | 80 | 79 | 17 |
| 16 | 92 | 91 | 90 | 89 | 88 | 87 | 87 | 86 | 85 | 84 | 83 | 83 | 82 | 81 | 80 | 80 | 79 | 78 | 16 |
| 15 | 91 | 90 | 89 | 88 | 87 | 86 | 85 | 85 | 84 | 83 | 82 | 81 | 81 | 80 | 79 | 79 | 78 | 77 | 15 |
| 14 | 90 | 89 | 88 | 87 | 86 | 85 | 84 | 83 | 83 | 82 | 81 | 80 | 79 | 79 | 78 | 77 | 77 | 76 | 14 |
| 13 | 88 | 87 | 86 | 86 | 85 | 84 | 83 | 82 | 81 | 81 | 80 | 79 | 78 | 78 | 77 | 76 | 76 | 75 | 13 |
| 12 | 87 | 86 | 85 | 84 | 83 | 83 | 82 | 81 | 80 | 79 | 79 | 78 | 77 | 76 | 76 | 75 | 74 | 74 | 12 |
| 11 | 86 | 85 | 84 | 83 | 82 | 81 | 80 | 80 | 79 | 78 | 77 | 77 | 76 | 75 | 75 | 74 | 73 | 73 | 11 |
| 10 | 84 | 83 | 83 | 82 | 81 | 80 | 79 | 78 | 78 | 77 | 76 | 75 | 75 | 74 | 73 | 73 | 72 | 71 | 10 |
| 9 | 83 | 82 | 81 | 80 | 80 | 79 | 78 | 77 | 76 | 76 | 75 | 74 | 73 | 73 | 72 | 71 | 71 | 70 | 9 |
| 8 | 82 | 81 | 80 | 79 | 78 | 77 | 77 | 76 | 75 | 74 | 74 | 73 | 72 | 71 | 71 | 70 | 70 | | 8 |
| 7 | 80 | 79 | 79 | 78 | 77 | 76 | 75 | 75 | 74 | 73 | 72 | 72 | 71 | 70 | 70 | | | | 7 |
| 6 | 79 | 78 | 77 | 77 | 76 | 75 | 74 | 73 | 72 | 72 | 71 | 70 | 70 | | | | | | 6 |
| 5 | 77 | 77 | 76 | 75 | 74 | 73 | 72 | 72 | 71 | 70 | | | | | | | | | 5 |
| 4 | 76 | 75 | 74 | 73 | 72 | 72 | 71 | 70 | | | | | | | | | | | 4 |
| 3 | 74 | 73 | 73 | 72 | 71 | 70 | | | | | <70 | | | | | | | | 3 |
| 2 | 72 | 71 | 70 | 70 | | | | | | | | | | | | | | | 2 |
| 1 | 70 | | | | | | | | | | | | | | | | | | 1 |
| AGE | 10:0 10:1 | 10:2 10:3 | 10:4 10:5 | 10:6 10:7 | 10:8 10:9 | 10:10 10:11 | 11:0 11:1 | 11:2 11:3 | 11:4 11:5 | 11:6 11:7 | 11:8 11:9 | 11:10 11:11 | 12:0 12:1 | 12:2 12:3 | 12:4 12:5 | 12:6 12:7 | 12:8 12:9 | 12:10 12:11 | AGE |

*Table 7:* Tests B Spelling Ages (in years and tenths)

| Year 5 (44 words) | | Years 6 and 7 (50 words) | |
| --- | --- | --- | --- |
| Raw Score | Spelling Age | Raw Score | Spelling Age |
| <2 | <6.7 | <2 | <6.7 |
| 2 | 6.7 | 2 | 6.7 |
| 3 | 6.9 | 3 | 6.9 |
| 4 | 7.1 | 4 | 7.1 |
| 5 | 7.3 | 5 | 7.3 |
| 6 | 7.5 | 6 | 7.5 |
| 7 | 7.6 | 7 | 7.6 |
| 8 | 7.8 | 8 | 7.8 |
| 9 | 7.9 | 9 | 7.9 |
| 10 | 8.1 | 10 | 8.1 |
| 11 | 8.2 | 11 | 8.2 |
| 12 | 8.4 | 12 | 8.4 |
| 13 | 8.6 | 13 | 8.6 |
| 14 | 8.7 | 14 | 8.7 |
| 15 | 8.9 | 15 | 8.9 |
| 16 | 9.1 | 16 | 9.1 |
| 17 | 9.3 | 17 | 9.3 |
| 18 | 9.4 | 18 | 9.4 |
| 19 | 9.6 | 19 | 9.6 |
| 20 | 9.8 | 20 | 9.8 |
| 21 | 10.0 | 21 | 10.0 |
| 22 | 10.1 | 22 | 10.1 |
| 23 | 10.3 | 23 | 10.3 |
| 24 | 10.5 | 24 | 10.5 |
| 25 | 10.6 | 25 | 10.6 |
| 26 | 10.8 | 26 | 10.8 |
| 27 | 11.0 | 27 | 11.0 |
| 28 | 11.2 | 28 | 11.2 |
| 29 | 11.4 | 29 | 11.4 |
| 30 | 11.6 | 30 | 11.6 |
| 31 | 11.8 | 31 | 11.8 |
| 32 | 12.0 | 32 | 12.0 |
| 33 | 12.2 | 33 | 12.2 |
| 34 | 12.4 | 34 | 12.4 |
| 35 | 12.7 | 35 | 12.6 |
| 36 | 13.0 | 36 | 12.9 |
| 37 | 13.4 | 37 | 13.2 |
| 38 | 13.9 | 38 | 13.5 |
| 39 | 14.6 | 39 | 13.9 |
| >39 | >15.0 | 40 | 14.4 |
| | | 41 | 15.0 |
| | | >41 | >15.0 |

# Examining the Results and Extending the Assessments

If the testing is to be of full value, the results should be reviewed systematically by the teacher.

The most useful initial step is to compare the list of raw scores with your own order of merit. If there are discrepancies keep an open mind, for it is when the test result differs from the teacher's opinion that it may be most informative. However, before more complicated enquiries are undertaken, check first that the difference is not due merely to an error in marking.

If the raw score proves to be correct, consider the possibility that the discrepancy may be due to the unreliability of testing. If the children are tested and then tested again on a parallel test, the average change in score is 2 for Infants and 2.5 for Juniors. In one case in 20, a difference of 4 or more for Infants, and 6 or more for Juniors, may be expected. If the accuracy of a score is seriously doubted, the simplest immediate action is to retest using a parallel test from the same bank.

Since the **spelling ages** preserve the order of merit obtained from the raw scores, they will agree equally well with the teacher's own order of merit. But they do offer more, since they make it possible to place the children's attainments on a scale derived from testing large numbers of children of different ages. For some purposes, teachers find spelling ages more helpful than quotients. For example: three Year 5 boys with quotients of 80, 85 and 89 had spelling ages of 6.9, 7.8 and 8.6 respectively. The quotients tend to obscure the different teaching needs which are more obvious when associated with age levels. Spelling ages are therefore more helpful for some immediate purposes, such as organising a suitable range of resources or grouping. Measuring *progress* on spelling age scales can, however, be very misleading.

Because they incorporate allowances for age, **quotients** are less easily compared with the teacher's order of merit, but they have the considerable advantages that have been described in *Using the Tables of Norms*.

In the following paragraphs, brief comments are made on the records of children tested at the end of Years 3, 4 and 5. The sequence of tests from left to right is: spelling age, then quotients for spelling, reading, mathematics, and intelligence (oral verbal type). The records illustrate the advantages of judging ability in spelling in relation to other abilities.

The first two children, A and B, are both poor spellers but A's difficulties are more general and there is no reason to be especially worried about his spelling.

B's difficulties in spelling and reading may not be remediable but the evidence of average ability in other fields suggests that some investigation might be helpful.

|   |    | SA   | SQ  | RQ  | MQ  | IQ  |
|---|----|------|-----|-----|-----|-----|
| A | Y3 | 6.7  | 76  | 72  | 70  | 74  |
|   | Y4 | 7.3  | 79  | 75  | 70  | 82  |
|   | Y5 | 7.6  | 79  | 81  | 77  | 79  |
| B | Y3 | 7.0  | 81  | 85  | 94  | 94  |
|   | Y4 | 7.5  | 86  | 80  | 100 | 100 |
|   | Y5 | 7.6  | 79  | 76  | 97  | 92  |

C is also a poor speller, being only a little better than A and B, but his difficulty is in sharp contrast, with distinctly above-average competence in other fields.

|   |    | SA  | SQ  | RQ  | MQ  | IQ  |
|---|----|-----|-----|-----|-----|-----|
| C | Y3 | 7.9 | 104 | 103 | 118 | 116 |
|   | Y4 | 8.2 | 96  | 112 | 111 | 121 |
|   | Y5 | 8.3 | 88  | 115 | 106 | 125 |

The need for further investigation of what appears to be a weakness in spelling (judging by the Year 3 results alone) is reinforced by the apparent relative decline in the course of two years.

As these examples might seem to encourage the fallacy that spelling attainment is dependent on reading and so necessarily falls below reading, D's results follow:

|   |    | SA   | SQ  | RQ  | MQ  | IQ |
|---|----|------|-----|-----|-----|----|
| D | Y3 | 9.9  | 123 | 102 | 97  | 99 |
|   | Y4 | 11.8 | 116 | 91  | 104 | 98 |
|   | Y5 | 13.4 | 120 | 96  | 96  | 99 |

There is in fact no reason why the number of children superior in reading should not be balanced by the number superior in spelling if the standardisations of the tests are correct.

The records of A, B and C show that decisions about action cannot be based simply on the present spelling ages. Although A is three years behind in spelling, he appears to be making progress commensurate with a wide view of his capabilities and no special measures are called for. By contrast C needs further investigation despite the fact that his spelling is 0.7 of a year better than that of A.

The underlying assumption is that it is valid to base our expectations on success in other fields. Though this does not always prove to be fruitful, it does nevertheless provide a way of deciding which children should be examined more closely. There has to be a choice. No class teacher has the time for extensive individual testing in spelling, reading, mathematics, and so on.

A specific weakness in spelling can be established only by showing that attainments in general are better. A comparison based on one other test result is not sufficient. For example, if the quotients for spelling, mathematics and intelligence are roughly equal, superior ability in reading alone is clearly not evidence of weakness in spelling. The average of other available quotients is the best criterion against which weakness in spelling should be judged.

|   |    | SA  | SQ  | RQ  | MQ  | IQ  |
|---|----|-----|-----|-----|-----|-----|
| E | Y3 | 8.1 | 104 | 125 | 114 | 123 |
|   | Y4 | 8.5 | 97  | 123 | 108 | 121 |

For child E a criterion quotient of 121 (the average of RQ, MQ and IQ) can be formed from the Year 3 results and, from the Year 4 results, a criterion of 117. The differences of 17 (121 minus 104) and 20 (117 minus 97) between the criterion and spelling quotients indicate a continuing difficulty, but how are the differences to be interpreted?

The following table provides a means of judging the importance of the differences. The table can be used either with a criterion formed by averaging reading, mathematics and oral intelligence quotients or averaging reading and mathematics of all Year 4 quotients places child E in the 1 in 40 category of 'very weak' spellers.

*Table:* **Evaluation of spelling/criterion differences**

Read the numbers in the columns VW (relatively very weak) and W (relatively weak) as '22 or more', '16 or more', etc.
RMI = average of reading, mathematics and oral intelligence test quotients.
RM = average of reading and mathematics test quotients.

| RMI or RM | VW | W  |
|-----------|----|----|
| >137      | 22 | 16 |
| 128–136   | 21 | 15 |
| 119–127   | 20 | 14 |
| 111–118   | 19 | 13 |
| 102–110   | 18 | 12 |
| 93–101    | 17 | 11 |
| 85–92     | 16 | 10 |
| <85       | 15 | 9  |

Since any class may be expected to have either none or only one or two children in this category, the procedure does not have to be applied very often. It is particularly useful if referral for specialist advice is being considered. Subjective opinions embodied in purely verbal descriptions such as 'a serious difficulty in spelling' are not a very secure basis for referral. And the term 'poor speller' is not very informative since it may be applied with equal force to the very different cases of A and C. Though A certainly would not be referred on this evidence, C might well be after further investigation within the school.

After confirming the results as suggested at the beginning of this section, what more can you do to clarify your view of the child's difficulties?

The child's test paper provides a useful starting point. For example, you may find that the child (at C's level of competence) has misspelt words like *yard* and has written *slipper* with one *p*. Such mistakes should be the basis of 'exploratory' testing in which the child is asked to spell words of a similar structure, e.g. *hard, card, mark, dark.* Such explorations, beginning with the easiest word misspelt, may reveal that some mistakes were isolated slips, but at some point the limits of competence will be confirmed and in concrete (as opposed to numerical) terms so that the teacher can plan a short-term teaching programme. This might, for example, cover the formation of derivatives by 'doubling' (*swim, swimming, pup, puppy*).

For this straightforward but valuable supplementary testing, it is better to use a spelling book with words grouped by similarity of structure rather than to rely on spur-of-the-moment recall.

You are advised to pursue the kind of diagnostic testing where the teaching follows fairly directly from the investigations, as outlined above, and to ignore the more indirect routes which lead to the classification of children according to types, e.g. as having 'weak visual memory' or 'weak auditory analysis'. Such classifications are of extremely doubtful validity and are therefore very uncertain guides to subsequent action. It is unfortunate that they have become unnecessarily associated with the analysis of children's errors. It is extremely important that you should examine children's errors very carefully in order to determine what needs teaching, but nothing is gained, and much of potential value may be lost, by over-simplification of the speller's difficulties. (See also the next section.)

Having examined the more immediately available information in the light of your own knowledge of the child, you will be able to decide what other questions are unanswered. Are there speech difficulties that are possibly related to the poor spelling? Is the child discouraged? Or do they just not care? Is lack of care evident in other aspects of his or her work? Is their handwriting slipshod? Are there careless mistakes in the child's arithmetic? Some of the answers to these questions are likely to be discouraging, but the questions should serve to remind the teacher of two fundamentally important points: any teaching programme must be planned to ensure that the child will have sufficient success to encourage further effort towards further successes; the content of the subsequent programme must be constantly adjusted to ensure this.

# Learning from Children's Spelling Errors

Children's errors are a guide to action so that the good teacher is constantly on the alert for revealing clues. Nevertheless, there are some ways of interpreting errors that are both time-consuming and unproductive, and which call for criticism not only because of a supporting tradition, but also because they are still being advocated in quite recent books giving advice to teachers about the teaching of spelling.

There are two kinds of error analysis. The first concentrates on what is written, the omissions of letters, insertions, etc. This is the method used in large scale investigations where there is no contact with, and no knowledge of the children as individuals. Such analyses are rarely of help to the practising teacher. The second approach tries to classify the errors in such a way that something is revealed about the speller. This can be illustrated by the following example. A common substitution for *with* is *wiv*. Viewed in terms of the first approach (the 'word-analytic' approach) this is a 'confusion'. In the 'child-analytic' approach this is a childish speech substitution with roots outside spelling. This view is more useful because it leads to consideration of what can be done. However, the 'child-analytic' approach tends to over-simplification and particularly to the over-use of categories such as 'weakness in auditory analysis' or 'faulty auditory perception'.

To illustrate his doubts the author re-examined (with other psychologists) Schonell's published case study in which '16 significant errors' were claimed to provide evidence for 'weakness of auditory analysis and sound-letter association'. But the evidence can be interpreted to reach the completely opposed view: that the wrong spellings show good auditory analysis, and that the sound-letter associations are defensible and consistent. Consider *cold/colled, talk/torck, seem/seam, folk/fock, remain/remane*. Other misspellings show inadequate knowledge of guiding rules (*bell/bel, fitted/fited*) and, possibly, lack of a 'model', for the spelling of two diphthongs (*noise/nose, spare/spar*). In two cases, the response seems to be dependent on partial recall of visual images (*worry/wory, through/though*). The other five misspellings are even less amenable to simple classification, and this is indeed what should be expected. When freed from preoccupation with concepts such as 'auditory weakness', the teacher can more easily surmise that this boy's difficulty lies in his mistaken dependence on auditory analysis and phonic spelling (with its occasional successes). If so, remedial work should concentrate on practising reliance on visual similarities in groups of words such as *cough, dough, rough*, etc.

Some analyses can be criticised from the point of view of the phonetician for whom 'auditory analysis' means something more definable than is evident in educational diagnosis. The following examples were easily found from a few passage-dictation papers: a child had written *strit* for *street*. The teacher's expectations for misspellings of the vowel in *street* are based on words like *weak, field* and *evening*. The phonetician knows that the vowels in *hit* and *street* are related and is, therefore, likely to be less surprised that the letter *i* has been used.

The teacher's expectations for misspellings of the vowel in *walk* are based on words like *more, pour*, and the less likely *wart* and *water*. But this vowel is related to the short vowel in *hot*, and the child who wrote *woking* for *walking* may have been showing better auditory analysis than might be initially granted.

Another child wrote *fratened* for *frightened*. His transcription (of his own speech) did not represent the short Southern vowel to be found in *hat* but the more open Northern vowel which is close to the first (and more important) element in the diphthong in *kite*. Since our expectations of the spellings of this diphthong are based on words like *kite, find, pie, dry, dye, eye*, the use of the letter *a* looks less rational than it possibly was for this child.

There are obvious reasons why alternative analyses cannot be asserted to be 'true'. The point of printing them is to discourage error analysis which disregards the many possible determining causes of misspelling.

One of the psychologically naïve aspects of ascribing errors to faulty auditory perception is that it overlooks the importance of central factors (attitudes, sets, expectations) that influence perception. When children (and adults) fail to understand the context fully, they find substitutes for some of the words in a search for meaning. For example, children who can recognise *southern* presented in one short sentence specifically written to stimulate the appropriate associations will sometimes respond wrongly to more ambiguous contexts. A dictated passage in which *southern valley* was used produced both *seven* and *sudden*. *Seven* was presumably determined by memories of the name of the Severn Valley, *sudden* by the same process of transforming the less familiar into the more familiar.

Note that the faults can still be classified as 'auditory', but this classification obscures the important fact that they may be more satisfactorily interpreted as being due to limited understanding of the passage. It is easy to forget that human responses are determined by far more factors than are open to observation and description.

Sometimes the misspelling itself suggests more than one contributory cause. A child whose other misspellings suggested speech difficulties wrote *wife* for *with*. Perhaps a first attempt *wif* was changed into *wife* because this matched visually with a memory of *wife*? The conjecture further emphasises the uncertainties of error analysis.

Dialect vowel substitutions are a further source of confusion. In some parts of England, *about* and *down* may be pronounced *abart* and *darn*, and, if the child is relying on spelling from sounds (rather than visual associations), it is his own vowels that are represented, not those of his teacher. This lends more support to the view that children should be taught by methods which constantly draw attention to the visual similarities between words despite differences in pronunciation.

The author is also doubtful about the usefulness of contrasted lists of so-called 'regular' and 'irregular' words as an aid to analysis. Lists of 'regular' and 'irregular' words suffer from the basic defect that what is irregular at one stage of learning is regular at another stage. For example, for the poor speller, *spoil* may be irregular. For a child with experience of *oil*, *boil* and *soil*, it is regular.

Error analysis can also reveal other aspects of spelling in which children's knowledge is lacking, and therefore indicate focuses for teaching. These could include:

- **spelling patterns for long vowel phonemes:** for example, misspellings such as *kit* (for *kite*), *wat* (for *wait*), *screm* (for *scream*) and *bot* (for *boat*) suggest simple phonic matching, perhaps using letter names. The child may be ready to begin learning the spelling patterns for long vowel phonemes.
- **words with inflectional endings:** for example, the misspelling *stopt* (for *stopped*) suggests that the child is not aware of *-ed* as a word ending indicating past tense; the misspelling *stoped* suggests awareness of this but not of the associated spelling patterns, in this case the doubling of the final consonant in certain words.
- **silent letters:** for example, the misspellings *sord* (for *sword*) and *wisper* suggest the child is unaware of the presence of silent letters in these words.
- **prefixes and suffixes:** for example, misspellings such as *rimind* (for *remind*), *punishmint*, *suddenlee* and *decorashun* suggest the child may be unaware of the spelling of common prefixes and suffixes, and/or of the idea of breaking a word down into its constituent parts.

Both the National Curriculum and the National Literacy Strategy Framework for Teaching emphasise the importance of knowledge of such spelling patterns and word structures. Identification and interpretation of misspellings related to them provides a firm foundation for sharply focused assessment and teaching.

# Construction and Investigations

The tests are primarily intended to provide a system of continuous assessment in spelling from Infant to Secondary level.

The graded word type of spelling test has many advantages. There are no seriously sustained doubts about the validity of the method, it is demonstrably reliable, and it has the practical advantages of being easily administered and quickly marked. It also has the further advantage of being easily adapted to the 'bank' system which introduces unpredictability into the content of the tests while providing matched tests.

There are further administrative advantages, from the division into a lower bank A (Year 4 and below) and an upper bank B (Year 5 and above): adjustments of the length of the tests do not have to be made to accommodate the total range of ability within a given age group and no estimated adjustments have to be made to the raw scores before consulting the norms.

Since the main purpose of the tests is normative, the items were drawn from E.E.R. Burroughs' *A Study of the Vocabulary of Young Children* (Oliver & Boyd) with no preconceptions about what the content should be. Because of this, the banks can be expected to achieve an unbiased proportional representation of the common spelling structures. Clinicians who have a preference for particular sequences can, with the bank system, select accordingly.

The advantage of Burroughs' study as a source is that it ensures that the majority of the words in the banks are within the understanding of at least some 7-year-old children. Other sources were used to extend the range to higher levels of ability, but 90% of the 576 words of the final selection are from Burroughs' lists.

The final warrant for the appearance of any word in the banks is not provided by its appearance in any previously published list, but that it has been found to have satisfactory discriminating power when used with English pupils in surveys of spelling and found to be suitable in achieving the designed range of scores. Note too the high correlations with other dictated word spelling tests whose content was presumably determined in other ways.

The above paragraphs outlining the rationale for assembling the banks can be expanded with a brief description of the procedure. All the words in the banks have passed through several trials to establish facility values and discriminating power.

The banks have been extended to their present size from a stock of items used in a series of unpublished standardised spelling tests and in the *SPAR* spelling tests. Items for which facility values were known were used to calibrate the new items in limited trials of groups of 120 to 140 words with 150 to 200 children. After a series of such trials in which the re-ordered items were moved to different trial groups, several such estimates of facility value were available, and items were used to form matched tests which were used in 79 schools and standardised.

Samples of the children's papers taken at four levels of ability were analysed, and the numbers of successes expressed as probits on graphs which, for each item, indicate both the discriminating power of the item and the facility level. By this means, the trials' statistics were checked by wider sampling. The items were then re-allocated to twelve matched tests for the final standardisations (1982). The pairing of the items has been further refined by a subsequent analysis.

An essential part of the bank system is the pairing, by means of which slightly easier words at any facility level can be balanced with the slightly more difficult words. This device has also been used for a specific purpose. To prevent any particular pattern or point of difficulty being over-represented in any randomly-selected test, words of similar structure (e.g. *climb* and *crumb*, etc.) which would have appeared in adjacent groups have been brought into the same group. The adjustments of the facility order have then been compensated for by the pairing.

The accuracy of the matching of the tests depends ultimately on the precision with which the facility values were determined. The matching process further reduces error. To check the equivalence of the five pairs of randomly chosen spelling tests used in the samples referred to in Tables 8–12, the five pairs of means were compared. The largest difference was 0.5 of a point of raw score which was not significant at the 5% level. As this check was prior to the final analysis and pairing of the items, it can be expected that the difference between tests has been reduced to insignificant levels compared with the more general sources of error variance to be tolerated in any testing.

The words have been presented in sentences to serve several purposes: the necessity of sentences is emphasised; *ad hoc* invention of possibly unsuitable sentences is discouraged; the time required for the preparation of a test is reduced.

The marking presents few problems other than those created by poor writing – hence the instructions to the pupils. Though reading capitals may have its advantages for markers, it was thought that asking children to use capital letters could adversely affect the spelling of those pupils who rely to some degree on motor-habits or the appearance of words in their usual handwriting.

## Standardisation

The standardisations of Tests A and B were based on the following main samples:

| Tests | Median age | Boys | Girls | Total |
|---|---|---|---|---|
| A | 7:0 | 209 | 212 | 421 |
| A | 8:2 | 409 | 352 | 761 |
| A | 9:2 | 399 | 400 | 799 |
|   |   |   |   | 1981 |
| B | 10:2 | 472 | 443 | 915 |
| B | 11:2 | 533 | 475 | 1008 |
|   |   |   |   | 1923 |

All the Junior samples were drawn from the same 19 schools selected from knowledge of their children's ability to be collectively representative of national standards. The Infant scores were calibrated by means of quotients obtained from the author's tests for Infants (1978, 1980a and 1980b). Table 1 is consistent with the norms in Table 2. The extrapolation of the norms in Table 5 to age 12:11 was consistent with the calibration of the scores of 196 Secondary pupils (median age 12:4) whose *Cloze Reading Test 3* quotients were available from testing at 11:2.

Comparison of the mean scores of boys and girls in the main samples showed a girl's superiority (in points of quotient) of 5 (Y2), 4 (Y3), 3(Y4), $2\frac{1}{2}$ (Y5) and $1\frac{1}{2}$ (Y6). The tables give equal weight to the boys' and girls' score distributions in constructing tables of norms with a standard deviation of 15 and incorporating an age allowance. The girls' superiority is therefore preserved in the quotients.

The spelling age norms were constructed from the tables of quotients – Tables 1, 2 and 3 for Tests A, and Tables 5 and 6 for Tests B. Equivalent scores obtained from the overlap of Tables 3 and 5 provided the extensions. These extensions were checked by using both tests with groups of children at 7:11 (N = 108), 9:8 (N = 88) and 13:0 (N = 86).

The age norms for Tests A and B were compared with those of the *Vernon Graded Word Spelling Test* (1977) by using this with Tests A or B. The median scores and spelling ages were as follows:

Sample 1 (N = 243): 12.6 *(A)*, 7.2; 12.3 *(V)*, 7.0
Sample 2 (N = 125): 19.9 *(A)*, 8.2; 20.5 *(V)*, 8.2
Sample 3 (N = 110): 29.5 *(B)*, 11.5; 40.1 *(V)*, 11.7

This shows a very satisfactory agreement between the norms of the two tests.

The following correlations were found in the investigations reported as samples 1 to 3, above.
1 (N = 243) *(A)* SD 7.2; *Vernon* SD 7.3; $r = 0.92$
2 (N = 127) *(B)* SD 8.2; *Vernon* SD 8.3; $r = 0.91$
3 (N = 110) *(B)* SD 11.9; *Vernon* SD 11.3; $r = 0.91$

## Validity

Spelling is important because it is one of the skills upon which efficient written communication must rely. Ideally, therefore, it would be most satisfactory if spelling could be assessed within texts produced by the speller. This is the test applied to adults writing reports for their employers, to letters of application and to purely social correspondence.

In school, the method is applied by teachers with broadly valid results; that is, three groups of spellers – the poor, average and good – can be formed without difficulty (except at the margins of the groups) and five or more groups can also be attempted with some success using purely subjective judgements. However, it is unfortunately the case that the method has limitations which prevent its being employed with anything like the precision that is provided by objective testing and, specifically, graded word spelling tests.

Young (1976) reported an investigation in which the spelling of 130 11-year-old children was assessed by means of two 30-word spelling texts (of limited range for 11-year-old children) and two essays written under examination conditions. The reliability coefficients were 0.943 for the two parallel spelling tests and 0.821 for the two essays. To obtain essay spelling marks of equal reliability to those obtained from one spelling test, three essays would have to be written and marked.

However, adults also implicitly accept another proof of spelling ability: the good spellers are the people who can correctly write the word that we require without reference to a dictionary, and there is no reason why this same procedure (as embodied in graded word spelling tests) should not be acceptable in view of the inherent difficulties in assessing children's essays.

The class teacher is not really faced with a choice between judging spelling from the children's writing *or* using an objective test. Objective tests have advantages that cannot be ignored (they produce reliable assessments quickly), while judgements of children's ability based on their writing will also be made in the course of teaching. When the two assessments coincide, nothing is lost: when the assessments do *not* agree, finding reasons for the differences may well be productive of new insights into the child's strengths and weaknesses. In other words, the teacher may find it profitable to regard *both* approaches as valid, and each as potentially capable of enhancing the value of the other.

## Reliability

Providing a context by means of a sentence helps children to be clear about what word is required but it is, of course, important that the tester should enunciate the words clearly and that the pupils should be familiar with her pronunciation. If not, the reliability of the testing will be lower. If the teacher is unable to make herself understood in the special conditions prescribed in the instructions, there should be concern about what is happening at other times. Again, examination of the children's errors suggest that what they write is a transcription of their own speech rather than that of their teachers, so that minor variations in the presenter's pronunciations are unlikely to make any difference. The satisfactory reliability coefficients of 0.943 and 0.933 reported by Young (1976, 1982) were obtained by re-test using two different presenters for each of the eleven sub-samples. These coefficients are practically indistinguishable from the coefficients reported in Tables 8–12 which were obtained from testing and re-testing by the class teachers.

The Tests A reliability coefficients for Years 2, 3 and 4 are 0.925, 0.956 and 0.936. The Tests B coefficients from Years 5 and 6 are 0.936 and 0.944. The average reliability for both A and B is the same, i.e. 0.94. The reliability of the test as established by re-testing using another selection of words is therefore very satisfactory and, on the evidence, unaffected by changes in the presenter.

The following table gives the standard errors (of measurement and estimate) and the mean differences for the scores and quotients of the samples reported in Tables 8–12. The statistics refer to both Tests A and B.

|  | Scores | | Quotients | |
| --- | --- | --- | --- | --- |
|  | Infants | Juniors | Infants | Juniors |
| SE(meas) | 1.6 | 2.3 | 3.7 | 3.7 |
| SE(est) | 2.3 | 3.1 | 5.1 | 5.1 |
| mean difference | 1.8 | 2.5 | 4.1 | 4.1 |

One interpretation of the standard error of measurement of 3.7 is that the chances are 19 out of 20 that a child's obtained quotient will lie within 7 points (either side) of his true quotient. If children are tested and re-tested, the expected difference between the pairs of quotients is 4 points.

## Predictors of spelling attainment

Future attainment in spelling is best predicted by present attainment in spelling as measured by objective tests such as the *Parallel Spelling Tests*. In one school, 82 children (43 boys, 39 girls) in three mixed ability classes were tested at 9:2 and again at 10:2. The coefficient of equivalence and stability was 0.918, which indicates a high degree of stability after one year.

If spelling ability is estimated by indirect means, the best single basis is reading ability. Tables 8, 10 and 11 in this manual and Tables 7 and 8 in the manual of the *Cloze Reading Tests* support this conclusion. The next best predictors are tests of mathematics and oral verbal intelligence. But any single predictor can be misleading.

If the 'verbal intelligence' test has to be read by the children it becomes, partly, also a test of reading and the correlation with spelling will be greater because of this, but then it cannot be claimed that it is 'verbal intelligence' that is the basis of prediction.

Examination of Tables 8–12 shows that the strength of the correlations varies from sample to sample. Although the samples were drawn from the same group of schools, the range of ability at different age levels is not the same throughout. This can be illustrated by comparing the sample SDs for reading with those of much larger and more representative samples: 7.9 (9.6, N = 1064); 9.7 (9.7, N = 761); 13.9 (15.3, N = 799); 15.3 (15.5, N = 915); 12.8 (14.2, N = 1008). The spelling/reading correlations vary accordingly.

# Statistics

These abbreviations are used in the following tables:
C1 = *Cloze Reading Test 1*
C2 = *Cloze Reading Test 2*
C3 = *Cloze Reading Test 3*
GMT = *Group Mathematics Test*
GRT = *Group Reading Test*
NRIT = *Non-Readers Intelligence Test*
OVIT = *Oral Verbal Intelligence Test*
SPAR = *SPAR Reading Test*
S1A and S2A = Non-overlapping spelling tests from Tests A
(No. of words as appropriate for age group.)
S1B and S2B = Non-overlapping spelling tests from Test B
(No. of words as appropriate for age group.)
Y1 = Y1 in *'Y' Mathematics Series*
Y2 = Y2 in *'Y' Mathematics Series*
Y3 = Y3 in *'Y' Mathematics Series*
Y4 = Y4 in *'Y' Mathematics Series*

## Table 8: Correlations
Correlations between raw scores (decimal points omitted). Standard deviations. Median age 7:2. N = 88. 3 Schools.

|      | S1A | S2A | GRT | GMT | NRIT |
|------|-----|-----|-----|-----|------|
| S1A  |     | 925 | 809 | 620 | 496  |
| S2A  | 925 |     | 828 | 593 | 456  |
| GRT  | 809 | 828 |     | 573 | 526  |
| GMT  | 620 | 593 | 573 |     | 649  |
| NRIT | 496 | 456 | 526 | 649 |      |
| SD   | 6.6 | 6.7 | 7.9 | 10.1| 13.1 |

## Table 9: Correlations
Correlations between raw scores (decimal points omitted). Standard deviations. Median age 8:2. N = 88. 3 Schools.

|      | S1A | S2A | SPAR | Y1   |
|------|-----|-----|------|------|
| S1A  |     | 956 | 911  | 681  |
| S2A  | 956 |     | 900  | 665  |
| SPAR | 911 | 900 |      | 739  |
| Y1   | 681 | 665 | 739  |      |
| SD   | 9.1 | 9.3 | 9.7  | 10.5 |

## Table 10: Correlations
Correlations between raw scores (decimal points omitted). Standard deviations. Median age 9:2. N = 91. 3 Schools.

|      | S1A | S2A | C1   | Y2  | OVIT |
|------|-----|-----|------|-----|------|
| S1A  |     | 936 | 740  | 559 | 486  |
| S2A  | 936 |     | 754  | 551 | 522  |
| L1   | 740 | 754 |      | 608 | 781  |
| Y2   | 559 | 551 | 608  |     | 679  |
| OVIT | 486 | 522 | 781  | 679 |      |
| SD   | 8.8 | 9.0 | 13.9 | 9.9 | 12.0 |

## Table 11: Correlations
Correlations between raw scores (decimal points omitted). Standard deviations. Median age 10:2. N = 100. 3 Schools.

|      | S1B | S2B | C2   | Y3  | OVIT |
|------|-----|-----|------|-----|------|
| S1B  |     | 944 | 864  | 718 | 695  |
| S2B  | 944 |     | 842  | 723 | 675  |
| L2   | 864 | 842 |      | 760 | 848  |
| Y3   | 718 | 723 | 760  |     | 717  |
| OVIT | 695 | 675 | 848  | 717 |      |
| SD   | 9.5 | 9.7 | 15.3 | 9.4 | 12.6 |

## Table 12: Correlations
Correlations between raw scores (decimal points omitted). Standard deviations. Median age 11:2. N = 110. 3 Schools.

|      | S1B | S2B | C3   | Y4  |
|------|-----|-----|------|-----|
| S1B  |     | 944 | 714  | 516 |
| S2B  | 944 |     | 713  | 538 |
| L3   | 714 | 713 |      | 662 |
| Y4   | 516 | 538 | 662  |     |
| SD   | 9.5 | 8.9 | 12.8 | 9.2 |

# References

DFEE (1998) *The National Literacy Strategy: Framework for Teaching*, Department for Education and Employment.

Freyberg, P.S. (1970) 'The Concurrent Validity of Two Types of Spelling Test', *British Journal of Educational Psychology, 40*, 68–71.

Hieronymus, A.N., Lindquist, E.F. and France, N. (1974) *Richmond Tests of Basic Skills*, Nelson.

Vernon, P.E. (1977, 2nd edition 1998) *Graded Word Spelling Test*, Hodder & Stoughton.

Young, D. (1973) *Oral Verbal Intelligence Test*, Hodder & Stoughton.

Young, D. (1976, 3rd edition 1998) *SPAR Spelling and Reading Tests*, Hodder & Stoughton.

Young, D. (1978, 4th edition 1998) *Non-Readers Intelligence Test*, Hodder & Stoughton.

Young, D. (1979) *'Y' Mathematics Series*, Hodder & Stoughton.

Young, D. (1980a, 3rd edition 1996) *Group Mathematics Test*, Hodder & Stoughton.

Young, D. (1980b, 3rd edition 1990) *Group Reading Test*, Hodder & Stoughton.

Young, D. (1982, 2nd edition 1992) *Cloze Reading Tests*, Hodder & Stoughton.